TOWARDS A NEW THEORY OF RELIGION AND SOCIAL CHANGE

Bloomsbury Studies in Religion, Space and Place

Series editors: Paul-François Tremlett, John Eade and Katy Soar

Religions, spiritualities and mysticisms are deeply implicated in processes of place-making. These include political and geopolitical spaces, local and national spaces, urban spaces, global and virtual spaces, contested spaces, spaces of performance, spaces of memory and spaces of confinement. At the leading edge of theoretical, methodological and interdisciplinary innovation in the study of religion, Bloomsbury Studies in Religion, Space and Place brings together and gives shape to the study of such processes.

These places are not defined simply by the material or the physical but also by the sensual and the psychological, by the ways in which spaces are gendered, classified, stratified, moved through, seen, touched, heard, interpreted and occupied. Places are constituted through embodied practices that direct critical and analytical attention to the spatial production of insides, outsides, bodies, landscapes, cities, sovereignties, publics and interiorities.

Global Trajectories of Brazilian Religion,
edited by Martijn Oosterbaan, Linda van de Kamp and Joana Bahia

Religion and the Global City,
edited by David Garbin and Anna Strhan

Religious Pluralism and the City,
edited by Helmuth Berking, Silke Steets and Jochen Schwenk

TOWARDS A NEW THEORY OF RELIGION AND SOCIAL CHANGE

Sovereignties and Disruptions

PAUL-FRANÇOIS TREMLETT

BLOOMSBURY ACADEMIC
LONDON • NEW YORK • OXFORD • NEW DELHI • SYDNEY

BLOOMSBURY ACADEMIC
Bloomsbury Publishing Plc
50 Bedford Square, London, WC1B 3DP, UK
1385 Broadway, New York, NY 10018, USA

BLOOMSBURY, BLOOMSBURY ACADEMIC and the Diana logo
are trademarks of Bloomsbury Publishing Plc

First published in Great Britain 2021

A catalogue record for this book is available from the British Library.

Library of Congress Control Number: 2020940543

ISBN: HB: 978-1-4742-7256-8
          ePDF: 978-1-4742-7258-2
          eBook: 978-1-4742-7257-5

Series: Bloomsbury Studies in Religion, Space and Place

Typeset by Integra Software Services Pvt. Ltd.

To find out more about our authors and books visit www.bloomsbury.com
and sign up for our newsletters

CONTENTS

FIGURES

PREFACE AND ACKNOWLEDGEMENTS

This book draws from two distinct research projects. Most recently I was involved in the REDO (Re-Assembling Democracy: Ritual as Cultural Resource) project, an international research initiative led by Jone Salomonsen and funded by the Norwegian Research Council. For my part, I conducted fieldwork with Occupy activists in London and Hong Kong. In Hong Kong, the work involved reconstructing the protest from the accounts of activists, whereas in London it involved documenting further protests and events that continued to be organized by Occupy groups, after the global wave of anti-capitalist revolt of 2011 had subsided. Before that, my Arts and Humanities Research Board (now the AHRC)-funded doctoral research and a subsequent research project generously funded by the British Academy's Southeast Asia Committee allowed me to work on alternative religiosities gathered around an extinct volcano some seventy kilometres south of Manila called Mount Banahaw. I conducted fieldwork with healers as well as small, independent churches and spiritual groups notable for their millenarian conviction in the imminent transformation of society, an interest in the accumulation and distribution of sacred power and potency (*kapangyarihan*) and their veneration of José Rizal – a Filipino novelist and doctor who was executed by the Spanish colonial regime in 1896.

The two research projects shared a number of features: first an interest in change, particularly of the sudden and fundamentally transformative type. Occupy activists and 'Rizalists' alike wanted to change their respective societies. Second, the two projects shared an interest in space. The Occupy movement was about the rupturing of urban space in the expectation of opening out alternative ways to assemble people together and to engage in creative projects. Similarly, the healers and churches in Mount Banahaw sought alternatives to what they perceived to be the unjust and immoral spaces of Manila, partly through pilgrimage to Banahaw's sacred spaces and immersion in its caves, waterfalls and healing waters but also through journeys along its hidden passages and to secret chambers and by building their own communities. By the time I was in Banahaw it was a veritable cottage industry of religious leaders, healers, mystics, pilgrims, New Agers and earnest research students, all participating in and adding to the Banahaw imaginary.

This book and its interest in change and space is very much a product of the work I pursued in Mount Banahaw in the Philippines and later with REDO, in London and Hong Kong. It is also the product of formal and informal inter-disciplinary conversations at the borders of the study of religions where the humanities, the social and the physical sciences sometimes meet, and it would not have been possible without the goodwill and support of so many colleagues and friends. I would like to thank Lalle Pursglove, Lucy Carroll and Camilla Erskine at Bloomsbury for their enthusiasm, support and encouragement for this project. To my departmental, school and faculty colleagues (past and present) at the Open University – particularly Hugh Beattie, Gwilym Beckerlegge, Marion Bowman, Graham Harvey, John Maiden, Suzanne Newcombe, Stefanie Sinclair, Helen Waterhouse and John Wolffe – but also Simon Carter, Peter Elmer, Rodney Harrison, Donna Loftus, Liz McFall, Jess Perriam and Peter Redman – I have an immense debt of gratitude: the collective mode of producing course materials at the Open University is something I have found, from the very beginning, to be a wonderful way of realizing a basic sociological insight, namely, that learning is both social and individual.

To my friends and colleagues who participated in the REDO project which contributed so much to the writing of this book, my thanks go to Tony Balcomb, Grzegorz Brzozowski, Gitte Buch-Hansen, Agnes Czajka, Grégory Delaplace, Cora Alexa Døving, Samuel Etikpah, Marion Grau, Ron Grimes,

Kjetil Hafstad, Ida Marie Høeg, Nina Hoel, Michael Houseman, Morny Joy, Jens Kreinath, Bruno Latour, Zaki Nahaboo, Birte Nordahl, Sarah Pike, Jone Salomonsen and Donna Seamone; it was an unbelievable privilege thinking with you.

There are others too who, along the way, have been the difference that makes a difference: Syed Mustafa Ali, David Chapman, Jay Cornelio, John Eade, José Francisco, David Garbin, Marie Gillespie, Suman Gupta, Titus Hjelm, Richard Irvine, Theodoros Kyriakides, Rebecca Lee, Chris Lewis-Jones, Magnus Ramage, Maria Nita, Francis Stewart, Steve Sutcliffe, Liam T. Sutherland, Sophie Watson and, in particular, my research students (past and present) Hilde Capparella, Owen Coggins, Lucy May Constantini, Alison Robertson, Aled Thomas and Claire Wanless. A final but very special note of thanks goes to Atsuhide Ito for enthusiastically throwing himself into the task of producing the wonderful diagrams for Chapter 3 and for the Afterword, 'Assemblage Drawings'. The photographs reproduced in the book are my own. For my family and for my friends outside the bubble – you are my constant companions. This is for Katy.

Introduction

The study of religions has long been dominated by modernity's double lens of reason and experience. Each lens entails fairly specific, methodological commitments tied in turn to particular definitional latitudes. For the lens of reason, religions are beliefs, concepts, views and ideas, best studied in terms of a realist epistemology recursively bound to the opposition of the natural to the supernatural. Accordingly, religions are cast as distorted representations of a real world, and those representations are destined to wither away as the operational or instrumental efficacy of ones arrived at, and continuously modified by processes of secular-scientific experiment and debate, become pervasive. For the lens of experience, by contrast, religions are practices, embodied emotions and affects where the emphasis lies on a hermeneutic and theology of moments, events and singularities tied recursively to a notion of the sacred as an opening or a rupture – occasioned by madness, possession or norm-bending effervescence – that radically de-structures the ordinary world to reveal something quite Other.

Each lens constitutes both a distinct vision of what religion is and a bundle of methodological procedures and rules for studying it. Furthermore, both are at work in the sociology of religion's two most cherished paradigms, the secularization thesis and the lived religion thesis. Each thesis seeks to model processes of religious and social change. The former has spawned numerous critiques and variants from the original, unilinear model of the decline of institutional religions in modernizing societies, including multilinear, oscillation and post-secular models; has crunched big numbers and been informed by ethnographic studies, the best of which take seriously the idea that modernity is multiple and not everywhere the same, and its effects on religions are, as such, far from uniform (Eisenstadt 2000). Nevertheless, at its core is a fundamental opposition of religion to the secular, the assumption that religion can be measured by recording (quantities of) expressions of doctrinally correct belief in populations and finally that such expressions will wither in modernizing societies. The lived religion thesis has also generated variants: religion is also implicit, vernacular and liquid, its institutional dimensions de-emphasized in favour of the spontaneous and the improvised. The focus is the ethnographic description of religious lives which are revealed not as bearers of orthodoxy or carriers of theologically correct beliefs but as messy, intractable and characterized by processes of mixing and improvising, with whatever bits and pieces of religions and cultures come to hand.

The theses form a complementary pair: one stressing religious decline; the other, religious production or creation. They are the field's defining accounts of religion and social change and, despite their quite different assumptions and conclusions, they nevertheless share the rational choice-making, meaning-endowing, individual human subject at their core and as a common site of analysis. The imaginary of a unitary subject as a site of belief and meaning and as a locus of action, underpins standard social-scientific accounts of religion: secularization is measured, after all, in the responses of this subject to interviews and to questionnaires concerning questions of belief. Likewise, lived religion claims the innovative and even heroic powers of this self-same, phenomenologically authentic individual subject to renew itself in a continuous process of religious (and neo-liberal) auto-creation.

As disciplinary approaches to the question of religion and social change they are of course perfectly valid, but what would the question of religion and social change look like if a non-, anti- or post-humanist point of departure was adopted instead? This book outlines an answer disrupting the sovereignty of the individual, human subject by situating it in a finely grained and thoroughly living, moving world of assemblages of human and non-human elements including (potentially) cities, the dead, ideas, institutions, monuments, mountains, radio and television, all of which, alongside the human, will be treated equally and without favour or special privilege (Harman 2018).

I take the idea of the assemblage to imply the spatial arrangement of 'heterogeneous, contingent, [and] unstable' (Collier and Ong 2005: 12) elements. To be clear, an assemblage is not a map or a diagram of a static if complex network but, rather, a complex and contingent articulation of human and non-human elements that actually generates, fabricates and produces new assemblages and, as such, is always on the move. An assemblage is 'a principle of connections' (Latour 2005: 13) with a generative agency that is distributed among its human and non-human parts.

Of course, thinking without the subject and with the non-human is not new but in recent years it has taken a new turn, away from structuralist and Habermasian critiques of the subject and subject-centred reason and towards a certain vitalism, and a recycling of the language of the nineteenth-century anthropology of religion notably (though not exclusively) that pertaining to animism and fetishism. Both of these terms were, in the late nineteenth century, rival theories for the origins of religion, and implied constellations of beliefs about the animacy or liveliness of objects and things. Importantly, their value today is not as indicators of beliefs but as principles of method: Arjun Appadurai's 'methodological fetishism' (1986: 5) and Félix Guattari's 'animist' subjectivity (Melitopoulos and Lazzarato 2012) – like Bruno Latour's (2010) notion of the 'factish' (a contraction of fact and fetish) and his claim that 'we cannot make a place for objects without modifying ... the social sciences, and without accepting a certain dose of fetishism' (Latour 1996: 236) – suggest a set of methodological assumptions about the real and the kinds of theories that might be deployed for understanding it (see also Haraway 2018). What these terms do is encourage an approach to religious and social worlds that does not begin with stable and immutable things and objects such as religion, class or society. Instead they offer flux, flow and transformation.

If there is a master science for studying religion and social change without the subject it derives as much from postmodern sources and the new materialism – both of which have been accused of trying to do away with the subject – as from the new, quantum sciences. Manuel Castells has suggested that sociologists need to look beyond their discipline for methodological techniques through which to explore new ways of conceiving the social field:

> We have an expanding field of the new mathematics of complexity based on notions such as fractals, emergent properties, autopoietic networks, and the like. Most of these mathematical discoveries remain confined to formal exercises with slight relationship to empirical research. But they are tools ready to be used, transformed, and perfected by able researchers with both the knowledge of the tools and the substantive knowledge to make sense of this formal language. (Castells 2000: 698)

In this spirit, Philip Ball (2004) has explored the extent to which 'physics is finding its place in a science of society' (2004: 3). If, in Newtonian physics, change boiled down to a strict causality – two particles collide like billiard balls to produce predictable, causal effects – the new, quantum physics privileges complexity, self-organization and emergence. No master algorithm or universal equation is sought, though that may have been Comte's vision for his 'social physics' (Comte 1998: 158). Rather, new concepts, methods and vocabulary offer new imaginaries for thinking about social and religious forms and how they change, from phase transitions to non-equilibrium bifurcations – terms which describe multiple interactions of elements and the tipping points between different states (compare with Tilly and Tarrow [2015] on repertoire transition, political protest and social change). One could begin with an historical example such as the 1789 French revolution, where one might want to plot the tipping point at which a solid, institutionalized religion (the Catholic Church in France) lost its structural integrity such that, by the 1830s and 1840s, a panoply of previously unthinkable religious experiments had either been tried or were underway from the Cult of Reason to the Cult of the Supreme Being, to the Religion of Newton, the Sacred College of Saint-Amand Bazard and Barthélemy-Prosper Enfantin, to the Icarians, and the Religion of Humanity. It could be argued that the heat of the revolution had excited the various particles of eighteenth-century French culture and society to such an extent that old interactions began to generate new things which, in turn, because those new things had been introduced and added to the mix, set off new interactions ... you get the idea. It does not matter that none of the experiments listed above survived for very long because the cumulative effect of those experiments was sufficient to re-wire the constitution of both the Catholic Church in France and French society more widely.

According to Carlo Rovelli, in quantum physics and chemistry, when two particles interact, something new is generated through that interaction:

> We have arrived very far from the mechanical world of Newton and Laplace, where minute cold stones eternally travelled on long precise trajectories in geometrically immutable space. Quantum mechanics and experiments with particles have taught us that the world is a continuous, restless swarming of things; a continuous coming to light and disappearance of ephemeral entities ... A world of happenings, not of things ... There is no longer space which 'contains' the world, and there is no longer time 'in which' events occur. There are only elementary processes wherein quanta of space and matter continually interact with each other. (Rovelli 2014: 31, 42)

When hydrogen and oxygen interact, water is formed. Significantly, water is a liquid while hydrogen and oxygen are both gases (DeLanda 2011). Does the quantum world of generative interaction offer a point of departure for thinking about religion and social change?

Maria Nita's timely *Praying and Campaigning with Environmental Christians* provides what she calls a 'snapshot of the climate movement' (2016: 227) in Britain between the disappointment (if not betrayal) of the 2009 climate summit in Copenhagen to the (tempered) optimism of the summit in Paris six years later. During that period Nita conducted ethnographic research with an array of groups from Christian anarchists such as Isaiah 58 to green Christians such as Operation Noah, participating in and observing climate marches, climate camps as well as workshops and related gatherings and events. Nita outlines an 'attractor model' (2016: 66) to describe the self-organizing networks of the movement and the entanglements of the various Christian and non-Christian activists involved in it. She represents the model through the visual metaphor of 'the spiral structure of a galaxy' (2016: 70) and with reference to the 'field of physics' (2016: 229), deploying these metaphors and ideas to try to envision the processes whereby secular and Christian groups coalesced together to participate in climate activism and in the process assemble new forms of religion, protest, culture and experience. In short, Nita alerts us to the collisions, frictions and interactions of climate science, political protest and Christianities and the extent to which these collisions, frictions and interactions generated new hybrid formations of religion, culture and the secular.

It is this general assumption – that interaction is generative – which forms the conceptual centre of this book. It might be argued that interaction is an apt metaphor anyway for the reality which the lived religion thesis seeks – through close qualitative analysis of lived religious lives – to make sense of. Perhaps. Certainly ideas such as *bricolage* aim to capture a general sense of play and experiment as individuals creatively configure and re-configure the different threads (or particles) of their religious lives. It is precisely through these acts and moments of wonder and creation that – or so the advocates of the lived religion thesis assume – the sacred is revealed. But the lived religion thesis has at least one insuperable problem: even if it is accepted that the thesis alludes to the kinds of quantum interactions suggested above, there is, for the most part, little or nothing sustainably or durably new that is created as a result, though their cumulative effects might yet generate more visible change. But the only thing that appears to survive lived religion's individual creators is the act of making itself, the knowledge of which is distributed anyway also among political activists, particularly anarchists, musicians and artists, and consequently its salience to religions and the sacred is, at best, ambiguous (Graeber 2007; Shukaitis, Graeber and Biddle 2007; Wanless 2019). Of course the lived religion thesis also assumes interactivity around a stable, central and organizing node called the subject, a move which keeps the interaction but controls or removes all the interesting and unpredictable, quantum bits.

It might equally be argued that the interactivity metaphor is apt for the reality that the secularization thesis seeks to empirically describe and analyse. Again, perhaps. The problem for the secularization thesis is not that it does not model the complex interactions of multiple particles (religion, individualism, the state, the market, Enlightenment, secularism and so on and so forth) but that the interactions appear to have no effect on the participating elements which are assumed to be real, irreducible wholes. As such, neither the religion particle nor the other particles are changed by their interactions; there is simply either less or more of them as a result. Again, the exciting part – the quantum part with its unpredictability and generativity – is tamed away to nothing. This state of affairs is not altered by Berger's initially promising paradigm of the two pluralisms – 'the pluralism of different religious options co-existing in the same society … [and] the pluralism of the secular discourse and the various religious discourses, also existing in the same society' (Berger 2014: 53) – which seems to set up the social as a space of interactivity between multiple assemblages. Ultimately, however, Berger seeks something like a special formula for managing interactions rather than for exploring their alchemical possibilities (see Berking, Steets and Schwenk 2018).

If methodological animism and fetishism, assemblages and generative interactivity constitute a point of departure for the study of religion and social change, what of religion? 'How do we make a disabling term', asks David Chidester, 'which bears ... [a] legacy of ambiguity, colonialism, and imperialism, an enabling vortex for thinking?' (Chidester 2018: 1). One way forward might be to think of religions in terms of forms and flows. Indeed, if the temporariness of religious forms is foregrounded then the focus of analysis can be concentrated at the moments of hardening and coagulation on the one hand, and at the moments of disintegration and dispersal on the other as a means of capturing – however fleetingly – the becomings and unbecomings of religions. There is already interesting research being conducted in this area (for example, Coggins 2018; Robertson 2017; Stewart 2017; Thomas 2019; Wanless 2019) which is opening out what can be thought of as religions precisely by complicating the boundaries of the term and by attending to the points at which religious forms harden and the points at which they melt, break down and begin to flow and take on new shapes (see also Gilhus and Sutcliffe 2013: 260 and compare with Bruce 2002: 199–203).

It might be argued that attention to form and flow is nothing new. After all, much of the history of the study of religions has been precisely concerned with a temporal procession of religious and social forms. The late nineteenth- and early twentieth-century fascination with evolutionary and developmental narratives of progress postulated successions of forms of religion and institutions such as marriage and the state, evolving through time. Animism, pre-animism, fetishism, magic and totemism were all contenders for the original form of religion, each imagined in terms of simple constellations of beliefs and practices that would be replaced by sequentially more advanced and increasingly complex arrangements. But these were forms already fixed and written by the hidden hand of Reason, set to appear and disappear on cue as each stage of human history was reached and surpassed.

As this temporal procession of forms gave way to a kind of patch-work quilt juxtaposition of forms with the triumph of culturalism, the question of change was either not asked at all or was simply referred back to a default narrative of evolution-lite, that is, as disenchantment, secularization and so forth. Either way, these forms – whether constituted within evolutionary or culturalist imaginaries – were assumed always and everywhere to be fixed, stable and coherent. What is emphasized in these pages are the flows of religions and the interactions from which new religious and social forms become and take shape.

The idea of forms and flows requires a further, spatial framing which consequently politicizes the analysis. Religions move or flow from one space into another, and these flows or movements are political to the extent that they presuppose borders, laws and states – sovereignties if you will – as well as wanderings, smugglings and disruptions. Indeed, they imply processes of sedimentation, coagulation and decomposition where solid forms break down and where liquids harden or ossify (compare with Tweed 2006) and which might, on a political spectrum, compare to authoritarian and anarchist social forms. If what I have written so far evokes the writings of Deleuze and Guattari it would be remiss of me not to acknowledge that there are numerous critiques of Deleuze and Guattari's work and one of the most serious, I think, is the charge that the privileging of flow and becoming constitutes an evasion of the political:

> The incessant flux of assemblage thinking … has the effect of reducing all historical struggles to abstract becomings. This move to abstraction empties them of their historical specificities, evacuates their meaning and their political force. Because it is also a universalising move, it *undermines* any possibility of alliance because it effaces difference in its specificity and therefore any capacity to negotiate it. Furthermore, in flattening difference, it effectively equalises all minoritarian subject positions and so fails to provide any critical resources to read struggles in relation to each other,

or to any political ethic beyond that of dispersion of power. (Conway, Osterweil and Thorburn 2018: 7; italics in original)

If politics and political struggle seem distant to the field of religion and social change, it is nevertheless the case that the historical and ethnographic examples developed in the pages that follow are deeply saturated by struggles against racial, ecological, gendered, political and economic forms of injustice. Importantly, neither religions nor the study of religions occupy some space above, beyond or outside the political and I hope that, in the pages to come, I am able to argue convincingly that thinking with flow and without the subject enables a deeper grasp of the political rather than its disavowal.

Approaching religion and social change in terms of methodological animism, assemblages, generative interactions, flows and spaces does not enable the discernment of the direction of change – it is not a theory with a predictive dimension. It is a rejection of subject-centred accounts of religion and social change inspired by Deleuze and Guattari's account of 'nomad' or 'minor' science and 'royal' or 'major' science (2014: 420–36). The spatial register of the 'nomad' is of course significant: the sovereign territory of royal science is traversed in a certain way to produce a certain point of view (see Scott 1998). Royal science, after all, seeks to authorize laws, axioms and theorems – to legislate the quiescence of the object before the all-powerful gaze of the sovereign, knowing subject. Nomad science, by contrast, 'rather than being a theory of solids treating fluids as a special case' (Deleuze and Guattari 2014: 421), attends to the disruptive flows essential both to processes of assembly and formation on the one hand, and de-sedimentation and disintegration on the other:

While minor science concerns itself with flows, major science treats fluids as a special case of a theory of solids; that while minor science deals with becoming, major science concerns itself with what is stable, eternal, identical, and constant; and that while major science prefers uniform or laminar flows, minor science is fascinated by the spirals and vortices that form when an inclined plane makes a fluid cross intensive thresholds, giving rise to convection and turbulence. (DeLanda 2016: 96)

One might be tempted to cast the sociology of secularization – which insists on the slow dissolution of religion from solid to liquid to gas and onto airy nothing, and the sociology of lived religion which insists not dissimilarly that there is no religion only a flow of *bricolage*-like acts of religio-cultural assembly (Davidman 2007: 54–60; McGuire 2008: 195–96) – as nomad sciences. Maybe so. Perhaps it is only their status as sovereign paradigms that make them appear as the enemy of the nomad. What can be said with certainty is that, following Deleuze and Guattari, a nomad science of religions will begin by giving free rein to five interlocking, methodological assumptions:

- assemblage and generative interaction thinking de-centres the rational-choice making and meaning-endowing, human subject by assuming the equal agency of the human and the non-human, in the process producing richer descriptions of religious and social worlds;

- assemblage and generative interactivity thinking focuses on moments of gathering and formation and moments of disruption and breakdown: it approaches social and religious worlds as aggregates, combinations and flows, aggregates, combinations and flows that are assumed to have generative and agentive capacities;

- assemblage and generative interactivity thinking attends to processes of de- and re-territorialization and to the spatial flows of bodies and things and the shaping and stratifying of spaces;

- assemblage and generative interactivity thinking deconstructs sovereign concepts such as Religion (with a capital R) inviting reconsideration of their insides and outsides, experimenting with alternative ways of drawing and un-drawing their borders;

- assemblage and generative interactivity thinking is empirical, realist and materialist: that is, it specifies dynamic assemblages of elements and situates them spatially and historically with space conceived not as a passive container but as a fundamental element.

Of course the problem with change is that it has neither a beginning nor an end. However it is approached, it inevitably seeps away in every direction, undermining any vantage point. Just as there can be no beginning point for the study of change so there can be no end to it either. Change is everywhere, and isolating it for analysis can only be a highly artificial and speculative endeavour. It cannot be carried out according to the Cartesian principle of breaking the problem down into its tiniest constituent parts in order to find direct, distinct and specific causalities, as that will only ultimately disaggregate and disconnect elements that, precisely because the object of study is change, must be viewed together. But if elements need to be viewed holistically as connected along myriad agentive and fibrous tissues and threads, there arises the question of the spatial scale of the phenomenon being investigated (does it span, for example, local, national and global interactions?) and its temporal duration (change is inevitably temporal but appears to flow infinitely in all directions, rippling sideways, backwards and forwards, thus requiring the artificial isolation of units or snapshots of concentrated time). The idea of the assemblage at least has the virtue of enabling the analysis of a manageable constellation of elements with an empirically specifiable spatial and temporal scale. Each assemblage, to be sure, when taken by itself, reveals little about change. But, by making use of the assemblage as a kind of map and by comparing and overlaying assemblages, I show how religious and social change proceeds not as the result of actions by human agents nor in terms of any speculative teleology, but rather in terms of the agency of assemblages of human and non-human elements in their energized flows and generative interactions.

The chapters

Chapter 1, 'Energy', proceeds along two, unequally weighted tracks. The first part of the chapter addresses that neglected current of social theory concerned with energy and society. It is a current – or a discourse – that oscillates between anticipations of growth and expansion on the one hand, and decline and exhaustion, on the other. The writings of Jean Baudrillard, Mircea Eliade, Claude Lévi-Strauss, Max Weber and Leslie A. White form a generative *milieu* to the later juxtaposition of Émile Durkheim's account of ritual effervescence with Jane Bennett's vitalism or methodological animism, which forms the basis of an analysis of a political protest and an investigation into the political agency of protest material culture. As such, the second part of the chapter builds from research conducted in London in 2011 and Hong Kong in 2013 on the Occupy camps that were established in each city. I develop a methodologically animist analysis of a moment of political protest in London in 2014 by the Occupy Democracy group, concentrating on a confrontation between an assemblage of protestors and protest objects on the one hand, and an assemblage of monuments and buildings at the protest site guarded by heritage wardens and police, on the other. My focus on the political agency of protest objects and things is not a cheap trick whereby the metaphysics of the subject is replaced by the metaphysics of the object: rather, it provides a means to introduce into political science and social movement discourses a language derived with some irony from the anthropology of religions, namely, one of animacy, ritual, iconoclasm and totemism, blurring the boundaries of religion and the secular and making the point that political agency flows from non-human sources too.

Chapter 2, 'Biology', explores two configurations of a biological imagination operative in the late nineteenth- and early twentieth-century anthropology of religion on the one hand, and the late twentieth- and early twenty-first-century anthropology and psychology of religion, on the other. For both, biology serves as an anchoring point aiming to calcify the idea of Religion (very much with a capital R), by giving it solid borders and fixed traits. However, by drawing from the work of Gilles Deleuze and Félix Guattari (2014) I add an alternative biological imaginary to the mix, one set in motion by their notions of the body without organs and the rhizome. This imaginary does an opposite kind of work, replacing calcification with flow and solidity with porosity, to open out Religion as something that is always on the move and that takes new and different forms in different times and places. The chapter concludes with the Flores assemblage, a hybrid formation of *adat*, Catholicism, colonialism and mission, development, megaliths, nationalism, so-called traditional religion and tourism. The purpose of this example is not to exoticize a non-Western elsewhere but to delineate, as precisely as possible, the entanglement of a religion (Christianity) with practices and performances that might conventionally be understood to be outside the purview of the study of Religion and, secondly, to stress the plurality of simultaneous religious and secular identifications that productively disturbs the idea of religions as discrete traditions that enclose singular identities defined by beliefs in the supernatural. To pull at just one of the elements of the assemblage: are the Catholics of Flores members of an unbroken chain of Christian religious tradition or, rather, are they participants within a Flores Christianity that is exquisitely inseparable from the other components of the assemblage?

Chapters 1 and 2 share a particular attention to space. In Flores – as in London – space is not a passive container in which the flows of action unfold. Rather, it is an active agent through which particular configurations, constellations and assemblages of bodies and things obtain their gravity and are routed. In Chapter 3, 'Generative Interactivity' – which draws from fieldwork conducted in urban and rural field sites in the Philippines between 1999 and 2010, specifically in Manila, San Pablo City and Mount Banahaw, as well as library research using primary and secondary historical sources – the idea of space is developed further, with a particular focus on towns and cities as vital points of concentration for the movements and flows of religions. Indeed, as machines for the regulation of flows, cities have long been associated with Christian evangelization but also with conceptions of the secular and the profane, with demolitions and expansions, community and alienation, modernity and parochialism, informal settlements and suburbs, automated systems, spaces of assembly, circulatory networks of traffic, commodities, monuments and power, as well as the slow, non-urban spaces at the ends of the roads, railway lines and power cables that feed them. Cities, then, are perfect laboratories at which to explore religion and social change because of what they are and what they can do (Frichot, Gabrielsson and Metzger 2016):

> Cities teem with life forms, technologies, agencies, materialities and ecological associations and niches whose concatenations comprise a characteristically diverse 'more-than-human-politics'. Entities such as rivers, railway lines, urban forests, wild fires, weather systems, sparrow nesting sites, feral cats, air quality indices, bat populations and sewerage treatment farms enter into urban political life in multiple ways via emergencies, crises, disasters, new technologies (or the collapse of old ones) and experimental situations, through individual, local, national and international spokespersons and organisations. They become matters of concern that complicate, mediate and interpenetrate those of everyday humanist concerns – development, building, planning, health, consumption, leisure and tourism. The arrival of such objects creates new subjectivities, ecological sensibilities and politics with the realisation that the modernist blueprinting does not take place against an assumed 'neutral substrate', that this substrate is itself active, lively, fragile, powerful and connected in ways that matter more than we imagined before. (Franklin 2017: 203–4)

The liveliness and power of cities was well understood by Spain. Their efforts at colonial evangelization in the Philippines occurred very much according to the spatial logics of a city and town-building programme – as mandated in the Laws of the Indies – which they launched as part of a process of imperial territorialization. The city is the key to understanding the question of religion and social change in the Philippines particularly in the lowlands of Luzon where the Spanish colonial presence was at its most intense, and it continued to be a key engine for change for the subsequent American colonial project in the Philippines. The later emergence of instances of religious urbanization and romantic, arcadian and anti-urban performances at the peripheries of the towns and cities and of the archipelago further attest to the centrality of the city as an imaginary for change up and down the country. By attending to the 'spatial models', 'morphologies', 'flows', centres and 'peripheries', 'place-making' practices and 'connections or disconnections' (Garbin and Strhan 2017: 11) enabled by the city, I trace the moments that solid Religion becomes liquid through the generative interactions of a set of four, Christo-Filipino assemblages.

Chapter 3, then, is interested in exploring the specifics of religious and social change in the Philippines. The chapter begins by exploring two theories of change in which human agency is explicitly positioned to one side – that is, Marxism and structuralism – as potential openings towards a new, general theory of religion and social change. Then the four assemblages are specified in such a way that change can be understood to be a dynamic property of the assemblages themselves.

The first assemblage emerged around the Laws of the Indies which authorized the construction of towns and cities across the Philippine archipelago and which was the key driver of Christianization: I call it the Philippines 1593 church-plaza assemblage, 1593 being the year the city of Manila was enclosed by walls to form the Intramuros (Andaya 1999: 19). Filipinos were relocated from their dispersed settlements and concentrated in the towns and cities as part of a process of colonial boundary-making: beyond the evangelized and panoptic gaze of the town and city insides were the hills and forests, the yet-to-be-Christianized spaces of the outside. The new towns and cities not only established this new inside-outside boundary; they also regulated the flows and movements of objects and bodies through its racialized and gendered membranes, establishing the pattern from which the three subsequent assemblages derive their urban spatial and transformative logic.[1]

The second assemblage pulses from an extinct volcano: I call it the Philippines 1841 Banahaw assemblage. It is an episodic assemblage distributed temporally from 1841 to the present at a single but paradigmatic site. It begins with the Cofradia de San José, an uprising which made its final stand on Mount Banahaw in 1841, followed in the 1950s by the construction of Rizal monuments in concrete by new, Rizalist churches and the establishment of the mystical city of God – the Ciudad Mistica de Dios – a moral community led by a Filipina whose father had been guided to Banahaw by the spirit voice of Apolinario de la Cruz who had led the Cofradia rebels to the mountain more than one hundred years before. The Banahaw assemblage, then, includes a ghost voice, vernacular appropriations of American urbanism and nationalist monumentalism and an experiment in religious urbanization among its component parts. If a map of this assemblage is laid over the top of the church-plaza assemblage it shows new centres of power in Banahaw at the periphery of the nearby towns and cities, and these new centres attract alternative flows of bodies and objects. These flows reverse the logic of the church-plaza assemblage and coalesce around new socio-religious formations led by Filipinos excluded from the racialized hierarchies of the church-plaza assemblage and by Filipina women around a cultural discourse of female religious power, materialized in part through new, religious urban and monumental forms.

A third assemblage throbs in far-flung, rural backwaters and in the forgotten or neglected places inhabited by the marginalized and dispossessed. Born in part of a long-standing alliance between Filipino left-wing activists and theologians that began in the 1960s and 1970s, these places have generated an imaginary of the true Filipino and have become vehicles for a discourse of authentic spirituality. I call it the Philippines 1967 arcadian assemblage because 1967 was the year of the creation of the National Secretariat of Social Action (NASSA) under the direction of Bishop Labayen, which led to the adoption of increasingly critical positions by elements within the Church towards the state. The date also marks the beginning of a process, within the Church in the Philippines, whereby seminarians, nuns, priests and theologians began to explore a range of new political, economic and ecological perspectives. The assemblage continues and expands the trajectories established by the Banahaw assemblage except that this time the values associated with inside and outside that were established by the church-plaza assemblage are put fully into reverse: the towns and cities of Empire and modernity become the primitive backwoods, while the boondocks become the centres of authentic spirituality as part of a fully articulated spiritual critique of secular, urban modernism. This critique draws from post-Vatican II theology but is also enmeshed within contemporary Filipino discourses about the simple life (which rests on a straightforward binary opposition between rural and urban living, with the former given a positive value over the latter) and a contemporary Filipino theology of indigeneity and spiritual ecology.

The fourth and final assemblage is linked with the emergence of a new religion – the Catholic, charismatic El Shaddai movement – and has expanded due to the spread of mass media and a new schizoid urbanism: new walled or gated communities and securitized spaces such as malls have replaced the walls and enclosures of the church-plaza assemblage as the primary sites of Filipino urban life and experience, while diasporic and virtual flows of people and things mobilized through radio, television, social media and mobile phone messaging have established new local, national and global circuits of transmission and connection among Filipino publics. I designate this the Philippines 2009 media-church assemblage, as 2009 was the year that El Shaddai completed construction of its first mega-church – the International House of Prayer – in Parañaque City, just outside Manila. El Shaddai's mass rallies, radio broadcasts, television programmes and mega-church performances allow them to operate across both physical and virtual spaces, adding new scales of connectivity and complexity to our three previous assemblages, that fully blow open the tightly regulated flows of the church-plaza assemblage: this assemblage, when overlaid upon the others, re-routes all old flows and exponentially grows new ones.

Each of these assemblages forms a pattern with the church-plaza assemblage constituting the root, and when these patterns are overlaid, one on top of the other, a kaleidoscope effect is generated which reveals a changing sequence of elements as well as the generation of new ones, specifically new religions such as Rizalism and El Shaddai. Importantly, the changes appear to be the property of the assemblages themselves and the agency of interactants that include town-planning documents, roads, the voices of the dead, monuments, mountains, radio and television. It is to be remembered that the assemblages do not form a temporal sequence whereby one assemblage replaces the previous one: rather, they all exist at once and will continue to exist until their spatially articulated urban and transformational logic of insides, outsides, flows and solids, is exhausted.

Chapter 4, 'Emergence', revisits the idea of generative interactivity and addresses the emergence of a new assemblage – the Cargo Cult – from the interactions of a range of elements compounded together as a result of the colonial encounter in Melanesia, in which a cosmic geography constitutes the centre of the assemblage. I begin the chapter with an exploration of two theories of religious creativity that fall under the purview of lived religion. The first theory draws on Max Weber's conception of charisma, that effervescent explosion of energy and power that is so disruptive of quotidian experience that it augurs the arrival of the absolutely new. The second has been drawn piece-meal from Claude Lévi-Strauss's notion of *bricolage* and from the Russian literary theorist Mikhail Bakhtin's notion of dialogism by scholars of lived religion to explore everyday practices of borrowing, blending and improvising such as those described by Robert Orsi in *The Madonna of 115th Street*, who argues that lived religion is a kind of 'cultural work' (2002: xix) that engages the body and the imagination in a kind of 'religious creativity' (2002: xxiii).

At the heart of charisma, dialogism and *bricolage* – as they have been appropriated by the theorists of lived religion – lies the subject, the very entity which this book has set out to get beyond. As an alternative, the concept of emergence allows the re-envisioning of new religions such as Cargo Cults in terms that privilege the generative interactions that the colonial encounter put into play. If the appearance of the Cults was, at the time, explained in terms of tropes of madness and contagion, their re-envisioning in terms of emergence enables the mapping of an historically contingent assemblage of elements including indigenous religion and culture, embodied mannerisms, conceptions of time and change, the Bible, radios and the dead, among a number of others.

The final chapter, 'Towards a General Theory of Religion and Social Change', delineates the contours of a nomad or minor science of religions, that is, its basic assumptions and approach to the field.

1

Energy

Introduction

In *The Savage Mind* (1962; 1966), Claude Lévi-Strauss distinguished between 'hot' and 'cold' types of society. At first glance, the distinction appears to map comfortably with the binary classifications typical of the classical anthropology of primitive and modern social forms. For example, Henry Sumner Maine distinguished between relations of status and relations of contract, Emile Durkheim between mechanical and organic forms of social solidarity and Ferdinand Tönnies between the organic bonds of the *Gemeinschaft* and the contractual relations of the *Gesellschaft*. However, while Maine, Durkheim and Tönnies were thinking largely within a constellation of nineteenth-century concepts of modernity inflected by rationalism and romanticism, Lévi-Strauss was thinking with the second law of thermodynamics, entropy and the concept of energy. For Lévi-Strauss, pre-modern societies were self-sustaining totalities immune to the forces of history and change while modern societies were simultaneously restless, progressive and destructive.

Lévi-Strauss's exploration of the social through metaphors of energy was part of a small corpus of anthropological and sociological writings exploring intersections of energy and society that included the likes of Leslie A. White and Clifford Geertz among others (see Rosa, Machlis and Keating 1988). Much of this work was marked by the indelible stamp of evolutionist social theory that linked ethnographic observations of societal and technological difference to energy consumption, imagining, for the beneficiaries of modernity, a trajectory of limitless progress and growth. If Jean-François Lyotard, Jean Baudrillard and the post-modernists would later outline a very different account of progress, European and especially German scholarship – particularly that articulated between World War I and World War II – had already sketched a pessimistic account of modernity intensely inflected by vitalism, anti-scientism and anti-reductionism, for which the eclipse of religious and spiritual truths constituted an almost intolerable prospect (see Eliade 1959; 1969a). This work was intersected by tendrils of holism and romanticism and would also become interwoven with the racist and anti-Semitic ideas that prefigured the emergence of Nazi culture (Harrington 1996; Jones 2010). If Martin Heidegger, Tönnies and Max Weber articulated a shared sense of German cultural crisis after World War I, (now) lesser known figures such as Houston Stewart Chamberlain, Christian von Ehrenfels, Oswald Spengler and Leopold Ziegler engaged in a German search for renewal in notions of racial and cultural purity as the means of staving off the collapse of a mythologized Teutonic culture (significantly – given his influence on the study of religions – Mircea Eliade also subscribed to these views and his work stands implicated in fascist and Nazi imaginaries of cultural degeneration and spiritual loss [Cave 1993: 106–7; 1993: 112; Dubuisson 2006: 173–88; Frank 2006]).

Precisely because of their anticipation of religious decline, sociological theories of secularization are located at a kind of hinge between vitalist and romantic critiques of modernity on the one hand and fascist and Nazi anticipations of collapse, on the other. Weber's formulation of disenchantment as a process that promised the arrival of a time when 'there are no mysterious incalculable forces that come into play' and when 'one can, in principle, master all things by calculation' (1991: 139), augured the apparent reduction of the world to a series of instrumentally oriented forms of decision-making purged of empathic, sacred and emotional elements. Weber's disenchanted modernity seemed to promise a future in which mechanical relations of cause and effect had become the blueprint of human action and agency, the outcome of which was not merely the total rationalization of human affairs but their secularization as well. Bryan Wilson's definition of secularization captures this spirit of disenchantment perfectly:

> The decline in the proportion of their time, energy and resources which men devote to super-empirical concerns; the decay of religious institutions; the supplanting, in matters of behaviour, of religious precepts by demands that accord with strictly technical criteria; and the gradual replacement of a specifically religious consciousness … by an empirical, rational, instrumental orientation; the abandonment of mythical, poetic, and artistic interpretations of nature and society in favour of matter-of-fact description and, with it, the rigorous separation of evaluative and emotive dispositions from cognitive and positivistic orientations. (Wilson 1982: 149)

Weber's sociology of disenchantment, then, was more than a prediction of secularization: it was an anticipation of a wider exhaustion. At the end of *The Protestant Ethic and the Spirit of Capitalism* he suggested that modernity was 'bound to the technical and economic conditions of machine production which today determine the lives of all the individuals who are born into this mechanism', speculating that it would 'determine them until the last ton of fossilized coal is burnt' (2002: 123). Importantly for Weber, no amount of charismatic power or energy would be sufficient to forestall the inevitable running down of the system (Parsons 1949: 752). According to Eliade, this tragic course could be avoided through re-connecting with the sacred and embracing the 'life-force' (Eliade in Frank 2006: 31). As such, he characterized the study of religions as a series of 'propadeutic and spiritual techniques' (Eliade 1969b) and its methodology as an hermeneutics of restoration, whereby the 'total man' (Eliade 1969c: 8) might be returned to the spiritual truth and reality from which He had become alienated.

In the first part of this chapter I explore Lévi-Strauss's writings on energy, situating them within a twentieth-century European intellectual *milieu* where currents of evolutionist, fascist, vitalist and post-modern thought swirl and intermingle. It is to be hoped that the juxtaposing of Lévi-Strauss with White, Baudrillard and Eliade is sufficient for opening out the treacherous currents of that moment – it is not as if we cannot still feel those currents today – and its concern with growth and expansion on the one hand, and decline and exhaustion on the other. The second part of the chapter sketches the contours of two, very different accounts of energy and society that move towards an animistic formulation. To do so I turn substantially to the works of Emile Durkheim (1915; 1960a) and Jane Bennett (2010). Both Durkheim and Bennett are interested in energies and things, and their role in the constitution of the social. Durkheim's account of totemism describes how the release of explosive energies is enabled through ritual assemblies of human bodies and sacred objects, the violent force of which brings the totemic social into existence. However, it is also a tale of a particular kind of political subject which emerges through the externalization of thoughts, ideas and emotions into material form as signs, symbols and representations (Durkheim 1960b). By contrast, Bennett's description of assemblages of human and non-human elements in 'living, throbbing confederations' made up of 'energies', 'force[s]', 'pulse[s]' and 'charged parts' (2010: 23–4), conceives of energy and things rather differently. Her methodological animism – if I can call it that – means that, for Bennett, there is no distinction between the human and the non-human, and there are no subjects and objects or insides and outsides: rather, there are only constellations in space of human and non-human elements. Moreover, her account of energy shifts the conversation away from explosion towards something more constant, more gentle and more sustainable.

I put flesh on this tale of two energies with ethnographic research I have pursued in recent years on the Occupy movement, specifically a political demonstration in the autumn of 2014 in Parliament Square in London, organized by a group called Occupy Democracy (see also Tremlett 2012, 2016; Soar and Tremlett 2017). The demonstration was very much a rite-like assemblage of bodies, objects, ideas, sounds and emotions but was marked by the iconoclastic destruction of protest material culture by heritage wardens and the police. My analysis of the iconoclasm posits a confrontation between two, rival assemblages of humans and things. The first, thoroughly territorialized at the protest site, configures together an urban topology of monuments and iconic architectures guarded by police and heritage wardens who, like the tourists that every day upload images of the site to social media (#ParliamentSquare), curate it. The political agency of this assemblage of people, place and things is constituted through exclusion, specifically an exclusion that requires the removal and/or destruction of rival elements. The second is made up of the protestors and their material culture, but includes other geological and ecological entities as well. The agency of this assemblage depends on its ability to occupy the space and disrupt if not indeed displace the icons and monuments of the first assemblage. I contrast a Durkheimian or explosive version of the iconoclasm with Bennett's methodological animism, to offer an energized account of the political agency of protest material culture.

Energy, evolution and entropy

Discourses of progress have been shaped by a biological imaginary as I detail in the next chapter – but they have been shaped by an energy one too. Technological and material progress depends on the generation of energy and its consumption. For the likes of Herbert Spencer, 'the ability to harness more and more energy … lay at the foundation of the evolution of societies', such that 'societal advance and the differences in stages of advancement among societies could be accounted for by energy – the more energy consumed, the greater the advancement' (Rosa, Machlis and Keating 1988: 150). Yet, even after evolutionism's demise in anthropology and the rise of culture as an explanatory horizon, the search for 'laws' (White 1943: 340) to explain technological and other differences between societies, continued. For example, the twentieth-century American anthropologist Leslie A. White re-ignited interest in questions of energy by framing culture as a 'thermo-dynamic, mechanical system' the functioning of which depended upon 'the amount of energy harnessed' and the way that energy was 'put to work' (White in Moore 2004: 185; see also White 1943: 346). White argued that progress was a direct, causal consequence of technological innovation and, while accepting that societies and cultures condition or shape the reception and development of technology, he tended to regard such feedback negatively as a potential break on technological innovation.

To us in the Anthropocene, the flaw in White's culture-thermic argument is obvious enough: according to the second law of thermodynamics, 'energy, unlike materials, cannot be recycled', which means that 'there is an inevitable limit to usable energy'. Given that 'energy is the lifeblood of economic and social activity, continued inattention to its limits should be the source of serious intellectual and political concern' (Rosa, Machlis and Keating 1988: 151). Indeed,

The second law of thermodynamics states the universal tendency of all isolated systems to pass from more to less organized states; this passage is called 'increase of entropy'. Increase of entropy is, if considered within the confines of the given isolated system, an irreversible process; the system cannot 'on its own' return to a more organized state. There is an interpretation of entropy as energy, which must be applied to bring the system back to its initial condition. This amount grows unremittingly as a function of time flow. No isolated system can draw the required energy from its internal resources ... The only remedy against the otherwise inescapable maximization of entropy ... seems to be to break the boundaries of the system open to exchange with what was previously its outside, and unrelated, environment. (Bauman 1999: 47)

The work of the archaeologist Joseph Tainter (1988) is pertinent in this regard: his studies of societal collapse in the ancient world demonstrate on the one hand the diminishing returns of increased societal complexity and, on the other, the difficulties that follow in seeking to stave off entropic exhaustion:

More complex societies are more costly to maintain than simpler ones, requiring greater levels of support per capita. As societies increase in complexity, more networks are created among individuals, more hierarchical controls are created to regulate these networks, more information is processed, there is more centralization of information flow, there is increasing need to support specialists not directly involved in resource production, and the like. All of this complexity is dependent upon energy flow at a scale vastly greater than that characterizing small groups of self-sufficient foragers or agriculturalists. The result is that as a society evolves toward greater complexity, the support costs levied on each individual will also rise, so that the population as a whole must allocate increasing portions of its energy budget to maintaining organizational institutions. This is an immutable fact of societal evolution, and is not mitigated by type of energy source. (Tainter 1988: 91–2)

Lévi-Strauss's engagement with theories of energy and society was very much informed, according to Christopher Johnson, by the 'thermodynamic or informational concept of entropy' (Johnson 2003: 116). In *Tristes Tropiques* Lévi-Strauss proposed the name of a new science – 'entropology' – to study processes of 'disintegration' (2011: 414), asking rhetorically, 'what else has man done except blithely break down billions of structures and reduce them to a state in which they are no longer capable of integration?' (ibid.).[1] Elsewhere he contrasted two models of the social, recycling the classical, sociological distinction between primitive and modern forms of society to suggest that

> the clumsy distinction between 'peoples without history' and others could with advantage be replaced by a distinction between what for convenience I called 'cold' and 'hot' societies [*les sociétés froides et les sociétés chaudes*]: the former seeking, by the institutions they give themselves, to annul the possible effects of historical factors on their equilibrium and continuity in a quasi-automatic fashion; the latter resolutely internalizing the historical process and making it the moving power of their development. (Lévi-Strauss 1966: 233–4; 1962: 309–10)

The distinction between hot and cold societies was first set out in the essay 'The Scope of Anthropology' (1994a: 29) where Lévi-Strauss included an additional binary opposition to that of hot versus cold, namely egalitarian to hierarchical social structures (in an interview with Georges Charbonnier he also opposed clocks to steam engines as examples of distinct types of complex systems). According to Lévi-Strauss, cold, egalitarian societies required only a small amount of initial input energy to get them going. They were characterized by a negative feedback loop where 'information on the output of the system is fed back to its input, to ensure that subsequent output is maintained within a limited set of parameters', while hot, hierarchical societies generated energy through exploitation – 'differentiations between castes and between classes are emphasized unceasingly in order to draw from them change and energy' (Lévi-Strauss 1994a: 29) – and were characterized by a positive feedback loop where 'the system is subject to an exponential growth that knows no limits' (Johnson 2003: 123). In short, hot societies exploit their environments – colonialism and capitalism being examples of securing, by whatever means necessary, constant access to new sources of energy – while cold societies generate a steady state with their environment, thereby guaranteeing 'both a modest standard of living and the conservation of natural resources' (Lévi-Strauss 1994a: 28). According to Lévi-Strauss, this steady state is founded in 'a particular wisdom which impels them [primitive societies] to resist ... any modification in their structure that would enable history to burst into their midst' (Lévi-Strauss 1994a: 28; see also Clastres 1994; Deleuze and Guattari 2014) and in a 'deep respect for the forces of nature' (Lévi-Strauss 1994b: 319).

In two further essays – 'Race and History' (1994c) and 'Race and Culture' (1985) – Lévi-Strauss outlined his view of history as endless combination, articulating simultaneously a critique of progress and the perils of mono-culture. Arguing that history proceeds in 'leaps and bounds, or as the biologists would say, by mutations' (1994c: 337), he introduced the notion of chance to history via the image of the gambler, whose moves and choices depend on successive throws of the dice. This re-formulation of history as radical contingency allowed Lévi-Strauss to suggest that progress was not the preserve of certain cultures over certain others, but rather the product of luck and, most significantly, combination and coalition with other cultures (1994c: 356). In 'Race and Culture', Lévi-Strauss continued the argument, but re-formulated it in genetic terms:

Over thirty years ago ... I used the notion of coalition to explain that isolated cultures cannot help to create by themselves the conditions for a truly cumulative history. For such conditions, I said, diverse cultures must voluntarily or involuntarily combine their respective stakes, thereby giving themselves a better chance to realise, in the great game of history, the long winning series that allows history to progress. Geneticists now express similar views on biological evolution ... in the history of populations, genetic recombination plays a part comparable to that of cultural recombination in the evolution of the ways of life, the techniques, the bodies of knowledge, and the beliefs whose distribution distinguishes the various societies. (Lévi-Strauss 1985: 17–18)

For Lévi-Strauss, entropy was not a process that could be avoided. Hence the question, how to develop a culture that was sustainable and that did not simply drain the resources – by conquest, exploitation and consumption – of everything it touched:

The necessity of preserving the diversity of cultures, in a world threatened by monotony and uniformity, has certainly not remained unnoticed by international institutions. They must also understand that, to reach this goal, it will not be enough to favour local traditions and to allow some respite to times gone by. It is the fact of diversity which must be saved, not the historical content given to it by each era (and which no era could perpetuate beyond itself). We must listen to the wheat growing, encourage secret potentialities, awaken all the vocations to live together that history holds in reserve. One must also be ready to consider without surprise, repulsion, or revolt whatever unusual aspect all these new social forms of expression cannot fail to present. Tolerance is not a contemplative position, dispensing indulgence to what was and to what is. It is a dynamic attitude consisting in the foresight, the understanding, and the promotion of what wants to be. The diversity of human cultures is behind us, and ahead of us. The only demand we may make upon it … is that it realise itself in forms such that each is a contribution to the greater generosity of the others. (Lévi-Strauss 1994c: 362)

Lévi-Strauss suggested that although cultural diversity was preferable to mono-culture, blanket preservation of cultures was not the solution. Indeed, diversities which were the residue of previous collaborations between cultures might even constitute 'putrefied vestiges' threatening the overall health of the 'international body' and might need to 'be pruned, amputated, if need be, to facilitate the birth of other forms of adaptation' (1994c: 361). Nowhere did Lévi-Strauss indicate how such decisions would be made or on what criteria, except that they would be the preserve of 'international institutions' (ibid.).

The idea of the West as a catalyst of entropy coupled with the idea of pre-contact cultures as entropy-proof has been a constitutive motif of certain romantic, fascist and post-modern disaffections with modernity. For Baudrillard, technological prowess augured no limitless arc of progress. Deeply influenced by Durkheim's account of totemic society and its capacity, through ritual, to resist entropic implosion, Baudrillard assumes that entropy is circumvented in so-called primitive societies via the cyclical release of explosive energy characteristic of ritual and symbolic exchange (see Lotringer, Kraus and El Kholti 2007: 9; see also Bogard 1987 and Chen 1987). Modern societies, by contrast, are subject to implosive energies and, he contends, are reaching a point of complete exhaustion marked by a descent into simulation and the hyper-real. In *In the Shadow of the Silent Majorities* (2007) Baudrillard claims that this descent cannot be avoided because 'the basic temporal form of society ... is no longer that of a progressive, expanding or historical society ... Evolution has now not just slowed down, it has entered a phase of contraction in which whole new series of laws apply: a society in a phase of inward implosion' (Gane 1991: 130). Where Durkheim's account of the totemic rite in *The Elementary Forms* describes a mass of bodies coming together to generate a strange effervescent power or electricity, the opening lines of Baudrillard's *In the Shadow of the Silent Majorities* seems to have been deliberately composed to evoke that rite and its energies, except that Baudrillard places all of its elements into reverse:

The whole chaotic constellation of the social revolves around that spongy referent; that opaque but equally translucent reality, that nothingness: the masses. A statistical crystal ball, the masses are 'swirling with currents and flows', in the image of matter and the natural elements. So at least they are represented to us. They can be 'magnetized', the social envelops them, like static electricity; but most of the time, precisely, they form a mass, that is, they absorb all the electricity of the social and political and neutralize it forever. They are neither good conductors of the political, nor good conductors of the social, nor good conductors of meaning in general. Everything flows through them, everything magnetizes them, but diffuses throughout them without leaving a trace ... They do not radiate; on the contrary, they absorb all radiation from the outlying constellations of State, History, Culture, and Meaning. (Baudrillard 2007: 35–6)

For Baudrillard, the spiral towards implosion is irresistible, and has acquired a seemingly 'fatal speed' (Baudrillard 2007: 74). Moreover, the media – the functional equivalent of religion in modern societies, and the adhesive that is supposed to ensure that the centre can, in fact, hold – generates a reverse effect: 'Instead of intensifying or creating the "social relation" [they] are on the contrary entropic processes, modalities of the end of the social' (2007: 51). This *reverse energy* (2007: 69; italics in original) rests on the paradox that as information expands and grows, meaning contracts and collapses: 'information dissolves meaning and the social into a sort of nebulous state leading not at all to a surfeit of innovation but to the very contrary, to total entropy' (2007: 102).

For Baudrillard, then, modernity is approaching exhaustion and history has run out of steam. In the sociology of religion, the theory most indebted to the teleological temporalities of modernity's evolutionary optimism is the secularization thesis. The thesis predicts the terminal exhaustion of Christianity in the West and of religion more generally under the corrosive effects of an endlessly modernizing modernity. From the perspective of Baudrillard's sociology, the error of the secularization thesis lies not in its universalistic pretensions or in its unilinearity, but in its failure to recognize that the collapse in religious affiliations, identifications and belongings is in fact but one element of a wider process of exhaustion. It is not only religion that is in decline, everything else is as well: populations have not only stopped attending church, they have also stopped participating in politics and community life in general (see Putnam 2000: 72; Stiegler 2013; Tremlett 2020).

Intersecting evolutionist ideas of progress and secularization, and post-modern intimations of entropic exhaustion, are a series of presentiments of loss and collapse that combine fascist and Nazi conceptions of national and cultural purity, romantic tropes of nostalgia and vitalist ideas about energy, life and creativity with a certain, general critique of positivism and reductionism. The writings of Eliade arguably constitute a compound of these elements, and his influence on the study of religions has bequeathed a vocabulary in which Religion is associated in a metaphorical chain with conceptions of authenticity and experience. According to David Cave,

> [One] source of Eliade's view of authenticity came through his Romanian mentor, Nae Ionescu (1890–1940). Ionescu was a university lecturer, logician, metaphysician, and, for several years, editor of the newspaper *Cuvântul*. Ionescu's philosophical term *trăire*, 'lived experience', became the codeword for the intellectuals of the 'young generation', whose movement, consequently, became known as *Trăirism*. *Trăire* is an existential concept that means to live life directly, spontaneously, and to arrive at one's personal philosophy through concrete experience. One is not to come to one's philosophy by consulting philosophical tomes, especially those coming from the rationalism of the Enlightenment and Western European currents of thought. (Cave 1993: 106–7)

The primacy placed by Eliade on authenticity and experience bears the imprint of this influence. In frequent allusions to intuition and creativity –

damned by Dubuisson as little more than an 'apologia for all irrational and intuitive experience' (Dubuisson 2006: 184) – Eliade's work combines a sense of spiritual crisis that is both individual and cultural, but with the possibility of renewal through a restored connection with deep religious and ontological truths. In order for this restoration to occur, however, it is imperative to resist the 'interpretations of religious realities made by psychologists, sociologists, or devotees of various reductionist ideologies' (Eliade 1969a: 70). This is the heroic role Eliade foresaw for himself and the history of religions – to restore the self-styled 'total man' to the Sacred:

> It seems to me difficult to believe that, living in a historical moment like ours, the historians of religions will not take account of the creative possibilities of their discipline. How to assimilate *culturally* the spiritual universes that Africa, Oceania, Southeast Asia, open to us? All these spiritual universes have a religious origin and structure. If one does not approach them in the perspective of the history of religions, they will disappear as spiritual universes; they will be reduced to *facts* about social organizations, economic regimes, epochs of precolonial and colonial history, etc. In other words, they will not be grasped as spiritual creations; they will not enrich Western and world culture – they will serve to augment the number, already terrifying, of documents classified in archives, awaiting electronic computers to take them in charge. (1969a: 70–1; italics in original)

If Eliade's anti-reductionism 'has bequeathed a deformed and distorted conception of reason' as 'mono-logical, instrumental and as a form of domination', his hermeneutics have contributed to an idea of 'religion as some kind of irrational and overwhelming experience that can become the point of departure for the re-enchantment of the world' (Tremlett 2011b: 288–9). However, the study of religions is not a stage for self-styled great men to act out their messianic fantasies, but an inter- and trans-disciplinary social science.

In what follows I offer an animist analysis of iconoclasm at a political protest that marks a break from the progress: entropy discourse on energy and society mapped out above.

Occupy Democracy

On the afternoon of Friday 17 October 2014, activists gathered in Whitehall, London, for what was planned as a week-long occupation of Parliament Square. A general election was on the horizon (it was held on 7 May the following year) while 15 October was the anniversary of the establishment of the Occupy London camp outside St Paul's Cathedral in 2011 and indeed the occupation of over 900 urban sites in over eighty countries by the wider Occupy movement on the same day.

Occupy Democracy can be situated within the recent history of the so-called Global Justice Movement that has sought to contest neo-liberalism, a form of capitalism that is characterized, by the Global Justice Movement, in terms of the socialization of risk and the privatization of profit (Mertes 2010: 78). In the UK, for example, the official solution to the 2007–8 global financial crisis was found, by national political elites, in the use of public money to bail out the stricken banks. The solution effectively meant that the pursuit of private profit by global banks and other financial institutions would thereafter be underwritten by the British public. The legitimacy of this course of action was found in a discourse of austerity which re-framed the global crisis into an instance of national profligacy (too much money had been frittered away on public libraries and benefits for the out of work and the disabled) that could only be addressed through collective belt-tightening. Of course, the belt-tightening was hardly collective at all: the rich prospered at the expense of everyone else, while libraries closed and deprivation and inequality exploded.

Since the late 1990s anti-capitalist protests have been notable for their use of social media 'to build networks to share information, tactics, strategies of opposition, and alternative economic practices' (Mertes 2010: 79). Among others, Manuel Castells has characterized the Occupy movement in terms of the emergence of 'hybrid public space made up of digital social networks and of a newly created urban community' (Castells 2012: 45). The movement and the camps it inspired are examples of new territorializations of space that transgress the boundaries and sovereignties of the nation-state by occupying multiple physical and virtual spaces simultaneously (see Chandler 2007). Groups such as Occupy Democracy are, according to the parameters of this analytic frame, symptomatic of local and global fractures as state-level sovereignties and territorialities crack and as web technologies make possible the articulation of new physical and virtual territories. Importantly, the Occupy movement was more than just a vehicle for protest: the urban camps it generated were experiments designed to pilot alternative forms of political decision-making, exchange and place-making.

The Occupy Democracy protest was organized by veterans of the Occupy London camp seeking not only to mark the third anniversary of the global wave of Occupy protests they had been a part of, but also to try to launch a series of experiments in democracy through the staging of debates with politicians, celebrities, activists, academics and others, about issues such as austerity, fracking and the future of democracy itself. These debates were characterized by the discussion of points of view on the economy, the environment and democracy which, at that time, were rarely represented in British mainstream media and political discourse. Nevertheless, they unfolded in a manner familiar to democratic, liberal political traditions: a speaker made an evidence-based argument and a public had the opportunity to discuss, contest, reject or modify the points made by the speaker. If the proximity of this notably liberal conception of political reason to Occupy political practices is notable, so is the fact that objects were never far away both in terms of the materiality of the protest itself but also in terms of the space in which the protest unfolded and was performed, namely Parliament Square with its iconic architectures and monuments.

Activists had hoped that they would be allowed to stage their protest and the various events they had planned on the grass in the centre of Parliament Square, although they knew that this would bring them into confrontation with the police and the heritage wardens. However, they hoped that their explicitly self-declared peaceful and time-limited protest would be allowed to proceed without interference. Activists did spend a few hours on the grass in the centre of the square on the Friday night, but by Saturday morning they had been confined to a narrow strip of pavement on the south side of the square and to a narrow, raised grass area running down its eastern side, where they remained for the most part, for six more days.

FIGURE 1 *Occupy Democracy protestors take the centre of Parliament Square, 17 October 2014. Source: author.*

The focus of the analysis is the actions of police and heritage wardens the following day. It is worth noting that the Palace of Westminster and the surrounding buildings were recognized by UNESCO (United Nations Educational, Scientific and Cultural Organization) as a World Heritage Site in 1987, although Parliament Square falls outside the boundary of the site. Nevertheless, heritage wardens patrol the square. Heritage, of course, refers to sites or objects that are regarded as special in some way by national and/ or trans-national bodies and groups. The institutionalization of a uniformed corps known as heritage wardens who work in Parliament Square and who are trained in security rather than, say, archaeology or museum studies, assumes that, in Parliament Square, heritage exists as an already fixed and already determined quantity that must be protected and preserved. It implicates a number of specific streets, spaces, buildings and monuments in a British heritage and political imaginary. Following Harrison (2013), heritage may be tangible – for example, it can be thought of in terms of specific materials – but it may equally be intangible and relational. The basic starting point is surely that protestors and protest things are no more or less heritage than anything else in Parliament Square.

Activists spent much of Saturday waiting to be joined by what was rumoured at the time to be a sizeable contingent of black bloc anarchists and Kurdish activists who, that afternoon, were participating in a large Trades Union (TUC) march through central London. While the Occupy Democracy protestors waited, the heritage wardens – accompanied by police – circulated the fringes of the protest seizing unguarded placards and banners and destroying them. These actions continued throughout the morning and afternoon leading later to the destruction of two large towers brought to the square by activists who had carried them from the TUC demonstration to the square, and who joined the Occupy Democracy protestors to briefly re-occupy the grass at the centre of the square. The acts of seizure and iconoclastic destruction by the heritage wardens and police were justified legally on the basis that while

FIGURE 2 *Occupy Democracy protesters briefly re-take Parliament Square, 18 October 2014. Source: author.*

the protestors had the right to protest, they did not have the right to do so with accompanying forms of material culture such as banners, tents, placards, tarpaulins, camp chairs or, specifically, anything that might be viewed as a 'structure'. The police and heritage wardens were enforcing the Police Reform and Social Responsibility Act of 2011 (which was amended by the Anti-Social Behaviour, Crime and Policing Act of 2014). The use of this legislation in the policing of the Occupy Democracy protest has been well-documented in independent and official media (see Graeber 2014a; Perraudin 2014; Ram 2014; Rikki 2014).[2] While it is beyond the scope of this chapter to comment on the legislation itself, it is certainly the case that while the legislation is quite explicit about what it seeks to forbid – activists sustaining protests for long periods of time by erecting tents and other structures to protect themselves from the weather – it certainly is not clear that the legislation empowers either police or heritage wardens to seize or destroy placards, banners or towers, none of which would be any use to persons seeking to shield themselves from the wind, the rain, the sun or the snow. In addition, it is worth noting that protest objects and structures are by no means always treated this way: in 2008, English Heritage in tandem with the Peak District National Park commissioned a team of archaeologists to document the Lees Cross and Endcliffe protest camp because of the camp's implication in the history of a landscape that protestors had sought to preserve from quarrying (see Badcock and Johnston 2009). Moreover, the Disobedient Objects exhibition held at the Victoria and Albert Museum in London which ran from 26 July 2014 until 1 February the following year, displayed a collection of protest objects at a site more conventionally associated with high art (see Flood and Grindon 2014; Soar and Tremlett 2017).

In previous research on Occupy camps in London and Hong Kong (Tremlett 2012; 2016), my work involved discourse analysis of mainstream and independent media sources combined with interviews and workshop-style discussions with activists. Likewise, when I arrived at Parliament Square in the late afternoon of 17 October 2014, I was for the most part focused on what people were saying; for example, in my field notes I quoted Russell Brand who spoke during the afternoon of the 18th alongside Natalie Bennett (the then leader of the Green Party), John McDonnell and Michael Meacher (both of whom were, at the time, backbench, left-wing Labour MPs: John McDonnell is, at the time of writing, Shadow Chancellor while Michael Meacher sadly passed away on 21 October the following year in 2015).

Brand said that he had been in Zuccotti Park in New York during the Occupy protests of 2011, and claimed that 'politics, economics and spirituality' had come together in the Zuccotti camp 'for the first time since the 1960s'. Certainly, one of the areas I have been interested in is conjunctions of religion and politics. But it was not until sometime later that I realized that neither what people had said nor the distinctive but already well-documented use of horizontal process, as part of the broader conception of pre-figurative politics developed by protestors and radical thinkers and applied by the Occupy Democracy protestors to frame decision-making practices,[3] were as significant as the seizure and iconoclastic destruction of protest objects that occurred by and large at the fringes of the protest.[4] What follows is an attempt to theorize protest things and their iconoclastic destruction in a manner that marks a break from discourses of entropy and progress and places their animistic potential for energy and political agency centre stage.

Durkheim, totemism and the energies of things

In *The Elementary Forms of the Religious Life* (1915) – a study of Australian, so-called aboriginal totemism that is usefully read alongside E. B. Tylor's *Primitive Culture* (Tremlett, Sutherland and Harvey 2017: 2) – Durkheim focuses on ritual and, in doing so, develops a highly original and influential theory of religion. According to Durkheim, the 'primary object' of religion is 'not to give man a representation of the world' as Tylor had claimed. Rather, Durkheim frames religion as 'a system of ideas with which the individuals represent to themselves the society of which they are members and the obscure but intimate relations which they have with it' (1915: 225). These 'obscure but intimate relations' are organized symbolically: the totemic rite assembles individuals who come to feel that they are acted upon by some external force. However, this external force is not any religious being or power, but society itself metaphorically represented by the totem, the 'flag' or 'emblem' of their society (1915: 206).

According to Durkheim, aboriginal social life is marked by two distinct phases: in the first, small groups engage in subsistence activities largely independently of one another. In the second phase, these previously dispersed groups concentrate for the purposes of celebrating a religious rite. Durkheim characterizes the first phase of hunting and gathering as of 'mediocre intensity' and as being marked by activities unlikely 'to awaken very lively passions'. Life in the first phase is, as such, 'uniform, languishing and dull' (Durkheim 1915: 215). However, once the groups have come together, a transformation occurs:

> The very fact of the concentration acts as an exceptionally powerful stimulant. When they are once come together, a sort of electricity [*une sorte d'électricité*] is formed by their collecting which quickly transports them to an extraordinary degree of exaltation ... The initial impulse thus proceeds, growing as it goes, as an avalanche grows in its advance. And as such active passions so free from all control could not fail to burst out ... This effervescence often reaches such a point that it causes unheard-of actions ... They produce such a violent super-excitation [*surexcitation*] of the whole physical and mental life that it cannot be supported very long: the actor taking the principal part finally falls exhausted [*épuisé*] on the ground. (Durkheim 1915: 215–16; 1960a: 308–10)

For Durkheim this explosive 'effervescence' is the energy and the source of the social. Arguing that 'there can be no society which does not feel the need of upholding and reaffirming at regular intervals the collective sentiments and the collective ideas which make its unity and its personality' (1915: 427), Durkheim goes on to suggest that these periodically organized releases of explosive, ritual energy are also capable of sustaining modern, secular societies: 'Hence come ceremonies', he says, 'which do not differ from religious ceremonies, either in their object, the results which they produce, or the processes employed to attain these results' (1915: 427).

Durkheim was well aware of the ambivalence of energy, and its capacity to generate quite different effects to the solidarity-inducing ones he hoped for: in *The Division* (2014) and *Suicide* (1952), *anomie* functioned implosively as disorganization, disaggregation and disconnection, and as a kind of short circuit or misfire. Moreover, in the work of the *Collège de Sociologie* (Richman

2003) and perhaps particularly in that of Georges Bataille, Durkheim's conception of explosive effervescence was re-imagined as a transgressive and revolutionary energy:

> The College ... understood the sacred as the centrifugal force at the centre of any social group and developed a novel notion of [political] activism that entailed the unleashing of this force. Activism then was not simply a matter of forcing political change by practical means, but of playing agent or catalyst in setting loose an unstoppable infection or chain reaction. The College intended to spread a sacred 'virus' through the social body that would bring the full explosion of the sacred ever nearer. (Grindon 2007: 97)

The work of Bataille and the *Collège* points to the ambivalent reception of Durkheim's work (Jenks 2003). If the British anthropology of Bronislaw Malinowski, Alfred R. Radcliffe-Brown and Mary Douglas saw in Durkheim's *oeuvre* the promise of a science of institutions and of cultural systems, others saw, particularly in *The Elementary Forms of the Religious Life*, the transgressive, violent and revolutionary potential of energy and effervescence:

> Structural Durkheimianism highlights the submerged morphological forces, legal constraints, and abstract conscience collective (collective consciousness/conscience) that narrate the *Division of Labor*, the mechanistic interactions and associations that animate *Suicide*, and the functional determinism and epistemological collectivism suggested by *Rules*. The conservative Durkheim talks about stability, legitimacy, democratic law, and social conformity, not only as empirical realities but also as ideals for the construction of a good society. Radical Durkheimianism points to creativity, effervescence, [and] the need to explode routinization via passionate association and transcendent ritual. (Smith and Alexander 2005: 5)

However, central to Durkheim's account of totemic ritual and explosive effervescence is the role of objects, something largely overlooked by the 'renegade' Durkheimians. For example, throughout the *Elementary Forms* (1915), he makes a number of references to *churinga*:

> [The *churinga*] are pieces of wood or bits of polished stone, of a great variety of forms, but generally oval or oblong. Each totemic group has a more or less important collection of these. *Upon each of these is engraved a design representing the totem of this same group.* A certain number of the churinga have a hole at one end, through which goes a thread made of human hair or that of an opossum. Those which are made of wood and are pierced in this way serve for exactly the same purposes as those instruments of the cult to which English ethnographers have given the name 'bull-roarers'. (1915: 119; italics in original)

According to Durkheim, the *churinga* are sacred objects (1915: 120) with a range of powers including the power to heal the sick (1915: 121). There are also the *waninga* and *nurtunja*, constructions assembled from various materials that are used 'to mark the central point of the ceremony: it is about them that the dances take place and the rites are performed' (1915: 124). All of these objects are sacred, and their sacredness derives from the fact that 'they bear the totemic emblem' (1915: 126) and it is through these objects that, according to Durkheim, individuals come to see themselves as members of discrete totemic, social groups. At a minimum these objects function as visible markers or representations of particular social groups and, as such, they are critical to the constitution of social groups. Durkheim's analysis of totemism, then, assembles a complex network of bodies and objects, electrified together by a massive release of effervescent energy. This explosive force not only constitutes the social but sustains it and protects it from dissipative disintegration (Parsons 1949; Badia 2016). Objects are central to this process but primarily as markers rather than as animate agents: different totemic objects distinguish different social groups, facilitating the high-level integration of the social body which in turn is captured by sociological analysis. Durkheim's epistemological and ontological commitments reproduce the positivist sensibilities of the early twentieth century: society is rendered 'thing-like' (Bauman 2005: 362), that is, as an object which can be studied as any geologist might study a crystal. It is composed of active human elements (it is their 'surexcitation' that generates the effervescence) and inert material ones, and it is the behaviour and ideas of the former – imprinted upon the totemic objects – that constitutes the focus of the social scientist.

Durkheim's account of totemism as an energetic concatenation of bodies and objects does not only narrate the formation of the totemic social; it is also the story of a specific type of subject which emerges through creating external representations, signs and symbols:

> Collective representations originate only when they are embedded in material objects, things, or beings of every sort – figures, movements, sounds, words, and so on – that symbolize and delineate them in some outward appearance. For it is only by expressing their feelings, by translating them into signs, by symbolizing them externally, that the individual consciousnesses, which are, by nature, closed to each other, can feel that they are communicating and are in unison. (Durkheim 1960b: 335–6)

The totemic subject – if I can call it that – comes to recognize itself through the material representations it has made. This Hegelian formulation performs the primacy of spirit or mind over inert matter, securing a particular ontology for the social and for politics, in which objects and things are little more than passive vehicles for conveying human meaning. This ontology is reproduced in contemporary research on social movements. For example, in 'On the Phenomenology of Giant Puppets: Broken Windows, Imaginary Jars of Urine, and the Cosmological Role of the Police in American Culture' (2007), David Graeber approaches anti-capitalist protest as a kind of totemic rite or festival that assembles human and non-human elements and which is bound up with the release of powerful energies channelled through both the iconoclastic destruction of protest material culture and the iconoclastic smashing of symbols of capitalism and consumerism. Writing with the 'renegade' Durkheim of the *Collège*, Graeber focuses on the smashing of giant protest puppets by police and, working from research conducted over a number of years at American protests including Seattle (1999), Philadelphia (2000) and Miami (2003), he explores what he calls 'the symbolism of puppets' (2007: 376) noting that they are often targeted for capture or destruction by police, sometimes even before they appear on the streets. For example, at the Free Trade Areas of the Americas (FTAA) protests in Miami in 2003, Graeber recounts an eyewitness report which claimed that

> after Police routed protestors from the Seaside Plaza forcing them to abandon their puppets, officers spent the next half hour or so systematically attacking and destroying them [the puppets]: shooting, kicking, and ripping the remains; one even putting a giant puppet in his squad car with the head sticking out and driving so as to smash it against every sign and street post available. (2007: 390)

According to Graeber, a giant puppet – which is made from fragile materials such as *papier mâché* – is, quite intentionally, a 'mockery of the idea of a monument' and of the idea of 'permanence' (2007: 382). The absurd and giant unwieldiness of the totem-puppets, according to Graeber, conjures the imaginary of the festival, and augurs 'the recuperation of the sacred and unalienated experience' (2007: 396; see also Krøijer 2015), mediating the rite-like release of powerful, violent, Durkheimian energy. But, if ritual constitutes the totemic social through releases of energy amidst experiences of ludic excess, does protest offer anything more than the possibility of cathartic release or the temporary suspension of the quotidian in a fleeting experience of sacred solidarity?

> This, I think, makes it easier to see why giant puppets, that are so extraordinarily creative but at the same time so intentionally ephemeral, that make a mockery of the very idea of the eternal verities that monuments are meant to represent, can so easily become the symbol of this attempt to seize the power of social creativity, the power to recreate and redefine institutions. Why, as a result, they can end up standing in for everything – the new forms of organization, the emphasis on democratic process – that standard media portrayals of the movement make disappear. They embody the permanence of revolution. From the perspective of the 'forces of order', this is precisely what makes them both ridiculous and demonic. From the perspective of many anarchists, this is precisely what makes them both ridiculous and divine. (Graeber 2007: 408)

If Graeber's account of violence against objects is correct, the iconoclasms in Miami in 2003 and in London in 2014 were attempts by the police to destroy the representations of creativity and imagination that had been materialized by the protestors. What the protestors saw in their assembly and in their material culture was, according to Graeber, the 'eruption of the sacred through a re-creation of the popular festival' (2007: 396). The police, by contrast, saw something else entirely. The destruction of the puppets by police in Miami was, according to Graeber, part of a 'calculated campaign of symbolic warfare' (ibid.) intended to prevent the ideas represented by the puppets from spreading to, and infecting, the wider social body. If Graeber's Durkheimian account is correct, then, the iconoclasm at the 2014 Occupy Democracy protest in London can be conceived of as the destruction, by police and heritage wardens, of potentially dangerous material symbols that threatened the integrity of the urban topology of icons and monuments at Parliament Square. However, in my view this is only a partial explanation for the iconoclasm: the protest things were destroyed not only for what they represented or symbolized, but also for what they might do.

The quivering assemblage

Jane Bennett's *Vibrant Matter: A Political Ecology of Things* (2010) is an attempt to explore the constitution of the political – including that of publics and political agency – in unequivocally provocative, materialist and vitalist if not animist terms:

> For some time political theory has acknowledged that materiality matters. But this materiality most often refers to human social structures or to the human meanings 'embodied' in them and other objects. Because politics is itself often construed as an exclusively human domain, what registers on it is a set of material constraints on or a context for human action. Dogged resistance to anthropocentrism is perhaps the main difference between the vital materialism I pursue and this kind of historical materialism. I will emphasize, even overemphasize, the agentic contributions of nonhuman forces (operating in nature, in the human body, and in human artefacts) in an attempt to counter the narcissistic reflex of human language and thought. We need to cultivate a bit of anthropomorphism – the idea that human agency has some echoes in nonhuman nature – to counter the narcissism of humans in charge of the world. (Bennett 2010: xvi)

Where the Durkheimian social emerges through explosive releases of energy that must be ritually and cyclically re-ignited to ensure that the charge is never exhausted, Bennett writes of a rather less violent 'quivering protoblob of creative élan' (2010: 61) that is always already energized. Drawing upon vitalist ideas of self-organizing, animate matter, Bennett traces the genealogy of her vitalism through Baruch Spinoza, Henri Bergson, Hans Driesch, Gilles Deleuze and Félix Guattari and, using the idea of the assemblage – of 'living, throbbing confederations' made up of 'energies', 'force[s]', 'pulse[s]' and 'charged parts' (2010: 23–4) – she pictures the political as an 'interstitial field of non-personal, ahuman forces, flows, tendencies, and trajectories' (2010: 61) and as

> an ontological field without any unequivocal demarcations between human, animal, vegetable, or mineral. *All* forces and flows (materialities) are or can become lively, affective, signalling. And so an affective, speaking human body is not *radically* different from the affective, signalling nonhumans with which it coexists, hosts, enjoys, serves, consumes, produces, and competes. (2010: 116–17; italics in original)

The concept of the assemblage allows Bennett to re-think liberal, political conceptions of publics and political agency. This move de-centres both the agentive, intentional, meaning-endowing human subject and the rational, choice-making subject, such that publics can include non-human elements and non-human entities can have political agency. Using the example of a blackout, Bennett moves towards what she calls a 'congregational understanding of agency' and then to 'a theory of *distributive* agency' (2010: 20–1; italics in original) in which agency is configured as 'something distributed along a continuum' and which 'extrudes from multiple sites' (2010: 28). It follows that if political agency is also the agency of non-humans – of 'edibles, commodities, storms, [and] metals' (2010: viii) – then the 'appropriate unit of analysis for democratic theory is neither the individual human nor an exclusively human collective but the (ontologically heterogeneous) "public" coalescing around a problem' (2010: 108).

The opening question of Anna Feigenbaum's essay 'Resistant Matters: Tents, Tear Gas and the "Other Media" of Occupy' (2014) is, 'Can a protest camp speak?' (2014: 15). Feigenbaum takes Bennett's assemblage as a key point of departure, suggesting that objects are not simply signs, referents or icons exchanged by human actors symbolizing human thoughts and emotions. Rather, Feigenbaum argues that protest things and objects constitute 'intended and unintended elements of communication systems' that 'mediate and articulate politics' (2014: 16). For Feigenbaum, the focus on material culture does not reduce protest things to representations of human thoughts, but re-cognizes them as elements of 'broader systems or assemblages' (ibid.). She argues that 'object-oriented approaches' (2014: 22) can help direct attention to the importance of physical objects and structures in politics, helping to de-centre human actors from the analysis of politics and political communication (see Winner 1980).

As a footnote to my earlier description of the Occupy Democracy protest, it is worth adding that among the protestors was a group of women who had travelled south down to London to participate in the week-long Occupy Democracy occupation of Parliament Square. They had come from the Barton Moss protest camp near Manchester where they had been involved in a long-term action against fracking (the difficult conditions of the London protest were nothing to the hardships they had faced at the Barton Moss camp which included serious allegations of sustained intimidation and gendered violence by police [Gilmore, Jackson and Monk 2016]). The presence of these women drew into the protest assemblage of human protestors and protest things a range of geological entities including water, shale and gas as a reminder of the non-human publics – whose agency has so often been neglected and ignored – to form an ontologically heterogeneous political community.

This chapter took, as its point of departure, the neglected discourse of energy and society, contrasting conceptions of growth and expansion with those of entropy and exhaustion, mapping their implication in modernist, evolutionist, vitalist, romantic and fascist imaginaries in which the secularization thesis was so strangely implicated. It then opposed Durkheim's violent, totemic effervescence with Bennett's gentler vibrations of people and things to analyse an iconoclasm at a political protest, and to bring into view an animistic vision of energy and the political in which both publics and political agency extends beyond the human to objects and other non-human interactants.

2

Biology

Introduction

In the nineteenth century when the sciences first began to emerge, it was assumed that distinct methods were necessary to study on the one hand the stuff of the natural world such as amphibians, birds, fossils and trees and, on the other, the (allegedly) highest elements of human life and culture, such as the arts, literature and religions. Wilhelm Dilthey opposed the *Naturwissenschaften* to the *Geisteswissenschaften* – the natural sciences to the arts and humanities, and explanation (*Erklärung*) to understanding (*Verstehen*) – claiming that whereas the natural sciences focused on explaining laws of cause and effect between phenomena, the arts and humanities were concerned with understanding the special meanings and inner (spiritual) experiences of human beings that were held to lie behind all great art, literature and revelation (see Grondin 1994; Palmer 1969; Harrington 1996: 27). Dilthey, in common with the vitalists and phenomenologists, wanted to 'restore the imagination and creativity against the threat of the mechanistic' (Jones 2010: 7) to insulate unmediated lived experience from *Erklärung* and the allegedly stifling effects of the irrevocably reductive, scientific method.

These romantic and eminently humanist assumptions would prevail across much of the study of Religion – and arguably still do prevail – despite concerted critical interrogation of the ideological, political and theological dimensions of those assumptions, and the implication of this classically humanist division of the sciences in the production of particular forms of power-knowledge about Religion (see, for example, Asad 1993; McCutcheon 1997; Fitzgerald 2000, 2003; Nongbri 2013). With these debates in mind, this chapter articulates an alternative to Dilthey's humanism, and one way to make these methodological concerns visible is through what I am calling the biological imagination which, in the study of Religion, is characterized by multiple appropriations of biology for defining Religion and for conceiving of social and religious change. This chapter stakes out two configurations of this imagination as exemplars of sovereign science and will sketch an incipient third biological imaginary for a yet-to-be-realized, disruptive, nomad science for the study of religions for which religions will be flowing and not quiescent.

The first configuration of the biological imagination straddles a period encompassing the late nineteenth and early twentieth centuries and a small but influential group of British and French anthropologists and sociologists interested in thinking through questions of religion, culture and society via a biological lens. Emile Durkheim, James G. Frazer, Herbert Spencer and Edward Burnett Tylor together produced a body of work on Religion in which recourse to the biological via a concept of evolution became the standard means of demarcating the contours of their field. Of significance are their appeals to the biological and the assumption of it as a realm of fixed laws, and their expectation that the evolutionary development of biological organisms was not merely analogous but isomorphic with the development of religion, society and culture. For these scholars, religion was a distinct object which they characterized as a necessary element of the evolutionary process, albeit one doomed to increasing obsolescence and eventual extinction.

The second configuration of the biological imagination covers the late twentieth and early twenty-first centuries, and emerges from the growing popularity of cognitive and evolutionary psychological theories of Religion for explaining its unexpected persistence. Scott Atran, Justin Barrett, Jesse

Bering, Pascal Boyer, Stuart Guthrie, Jonathan Jong, Ilkke Pyysiäinen, Dan Sperber and Harvey Whitehouse, among others, have approached the question of Religion assuming its implication in the functioning of the evolved cognitive architecture of the human mind. For these scholars – and for new atheists including Richard Dawkins, Daniel Dennett, Sam Harris and Christopher Hitchens whose populist attacks on Religion draw substantially upon cognitive theory and evolutionary psychology – evolutionary theory has enabled the development of new concepts and seductive metaphors to explain how Religion survives even in modern ecologies still assumed to be hostile to it. For example, Dawkins has deployed the neologism 'memes' as a means of thinking about religious beliefs, their transmission and distribution in populations, while Dan Sperber's conception of the *'epidemiology of representations'* (Sperber 1996: 1; italics in original) significantly re-orients anthropological theories of culture and learning towards a disease model. Important too is the extent to which cognitive and new atheist theorists frame the subject: on the one hand, their humanist sensibilities must uphold Enlightenment ideals of reason and its hero of knowledge in the pursuit of rational knowledge about the world, an ideal, they argue, religious belief confounds. Yet, at the same time, cognitive theory's 'standard model' 'posits religion as a by-product of other evolutionary adaptations' (Jong 2017: 54) and 'religious thoughts' not as 'a dramatic departure from, but a predictable by-product of, ordinary cognitive function' (Boyer 2003: 119). But if religious thoughts are 'by-products' of other mental functions, does this mean that the thinking subject does not know or is not able to control its own mind? Whereas Durkheim, Frazer and Tylor understood Religion in terms of modes of thought and cognition distinct from those associated with the exercise of liberal reason, the cognitivist formulation frames Religion as an unintended effect of evolved cognitive mechanisms: the subject is little more than a container for the unwinding of hard-wired psychological architectures.

Significant too is the idea of a hierarchy of the sciences that is cultivated in cognitive theory, ranging from the most to the least scientific, and where the cultural, social, psychological and historical disciplines only attain status as sciences once they have been reconfigured through the lens of Darwinian evolutionary theory or, perhaps slightly more diplomatically, when 'researchers ... take advantage of the parallels between biological and cultural change to model a science of culture along the lines of evolutionary biology' (Mesoudi, Whiten and Laland 2007: 18; see also Tooby and Cosmides 1992; Ingold 2007a). Of course, neither cognitive psychologists nor new atheists reflect much on their science: no Thomas Kuhn (1970), Paul Feyerabend (2010), Imre Lakatos (1978) or, God forbid, Donna Haraway (1991a; 1991b), Genevieve Lloyd (1993), Sandra Harding (2004) or Linda Tuhiwai Smith (1999), for them. So, the experiment proposed here is to add to the mix an alternative biological imaginary drawn from Deleuze and Guattari's (2014) idea of the rhizome and of the body without organs.

Deleuze and Guattari's work refracts elements of so-called vitalism through post-structuralist French thought. Earlier forms of vitalism eulogized lived experience and railed against what was perceived as the mechanistic reduction of imagination and creativity occasioned by industrial, urban modernity. Vitalism bundled together conceptions of teleology, autonomy, self-organization, entelechy and the idea of a life spark, sometimes divinely ignited, against nineteenth-century scientism and capitalism (cf. Eliade 1969a: 70–1). Converging with post-structuralist interests in non-linearity and hybridity, Deleuze and Guattari's ideas have been influential upon the thinking of Jane Bennett, Manuel DeLanda, Donna Haraway, Tim Ingold and Bruno Latour, among others.[1] The body without organs and the rhizome suggest a counter-biology, a biology without a subject, a de-territorializing biology that deals not in hard essences but in flows, assemblages and contingent articulations. As such, I conclude the chapter with what I call the Flores assemblage, a hybrid of *adat*, Catholicism, development, megaliths, nationalism, so-called traditional religion and tourism. The purpose of this example is to demonstrate firstly the entanglement of religions with practices and performances that might conventionally be understood as outside the purview of the study of religions and, secondly, to explore the plurality of simultaneous religious and secular identifications that productively disturb the idea of religions as discrete traditions that define singular identities. To pull at just one of the elements of the assemblage: are the Catholics of Flores members of an unbroken chain of Christian religious tradition or, rather, are they participants within a Flores Christianity that is exquisitely inseparable from the other components of the assemblage?

'Darwinism makes it possible'

R. R. Marett's memorable phrase 'Darwinism makes it possible' (Marett 1912: 8) was an answer to the question, 'what is anthropology?'. For Marett, anthropology and 'Darwinism' shared the assumption that 'all forms of life in the world are related together' and that these relations were 'sufficiently uniform to be described under a general formula or law of evolution' (1912: 9). According to Eric Sharpe, one of the consequences of this assumption was that, where once religion had been understood as a 'revealed truth', it thereafter became a 'developing organism' (Sharpe 1986: 48; see also Cox 2006: 70–1), conceivable as something living, growing, changing and dying according to the same evolutionary laws of development, and knowable through following the same kinds of natural scientific methodologies that had been pursued by Darwin in his work about plants and animals in *On the Origin of Species* (1859). For Frazer, the theory of evolution was the foundation for a 'mental anthropology' which had emerged

almost immediately [after] the promulgation of the evolution theory by Darwin and Wallace in 1859. I think I am right in saying that the foundation of anthropological societies at home and abroad has everywhere been subsequent to that date and has followed it often at very short intervals. Be that as it may, the theory of the gradual evolution of man out of a long series of inferior forms of animal life is now generally accepted, though diversity of opinion still prevails as to the precise mode in which the evolution has been brought about. It is this conception of evolution which supplies a basis for the modern science of anthropology. (Frazer 1931: 235–6)

Certainly Darwin's discoveries opened up a completely new way of understanding the world, yet Durkheim, Frazer, Spencer and Tylor held views about religion, change and development that were hardly Darwinian at all, including the notion of linear, developmental progress that could be plotted along a single line. European thinkers had already postulated, in the mid-eighteenth century, a linear and sequential conception of history that challenged biblical ideas of degeneration from an originary state of perfection. By contrast, Darwinian evolution described processes of adaptation to unpredictable environmental shifts and random mutations, which meant that even if species had a common origin they would develop along endlessly bifurcating lines if and as they became isolated, in different environmental contexts (Kuper 1988: 3). Yet, Durkheim, Frazer, Spencer and Tylor saw themselves as evolution's heirs, charged with the task of bringing its insights to the study of society and religion and, as such, they did not regard their appeals to biology as being merely literary or metaphorical. By the same token, those appeals were imaginative, marked by sweeping leaps across domains of society, religion and nature which had previously been seen as separate and unconnected.

For Spencer, the appeal to biology was premised on the idea that social and natural forms might be explored by a single science. In the essay 'Transcendental Physiology' (1890a) he outlined a synthetic perspective aimed towards a comparative analysis of the structure of forms:

It is also becoming clear that the general principles of development and structure displayed in organized bodies are displayed in societies also. The fundamental characteristic both of societies and of living creatures, is, that they consist of mutually-dependent parts; and it would seem that this involves a community of various other characteristics. Those who are acquainted with the broad facts of both physiology and sociology, are beginning to recognize this correspondence not as a plausible fancy, but as a scientific truth. (Spencer 1890a: 60)

For Spencer, physiology and sociology were dealing with the same processes by which entities developed and, in his essay 'The Social Organism' (1890b), he proposed a series of analogies through which the growth of organic bodies could be seen as laying a template for the development of social and political bodies. For example, he compared the spontaneous divisions and aggregations of protozoa to aboriginal groups, the blood and the circulatory networks of living bodies to the circulations of commodities in modern societies, and the nervous system to telegraph and railway systems. These comparisons were clearly neither neutral nor simply comparisons: they were also rankings by which biological and social developments could be conceptualized through the politically charged lens of progress. Moreover, they allowed Spencer to confidently claim that across both the social and the biological realms, 'the principles of organization are the same' (Spencer 1890b: 164). For Spencer, society was not a product of human action but rather emerged out of a 'general developmental process' (1890b: 159) that shared with biology the tendency to assume, 'in the course of ... growth, a continually increasing complexity of structure' (1890b: 161).

Like Spencer, Durkheim took the view that the new sciences of biology and sociology were analysing processes that were more than merely similar in kind or lending themselves to metaphorical association. Durkheim's appeals to biology were, like Spencer's, premised upon the idea of a fundamental unity of biological and social realms:

The recent philosophical speculations in biology have finally caused us to realise that the division of labor [*la division du travail*] is a fact of a generality that the economists, who were the first to speak of it, had been incapable of suspecting. Indeed ... we know that the law of the division of labor applies to organisms as well as to societies ... This discovery has had the result not only of enlarging enormously the field of action of the division of labor, but also of setting its origins back into an infinitely distant past ... It is no longer a mere social institution whose roots lie in the intelligence and will of men, but a general biological phenomenon [*phénomène de biologie générale*], the conditions for which must seemingly be sought in the essential properties of organized matter [*la matière organisée*]. (Durkheim 2014: 34; Durkheim 2013: 4)

Biology offered not only a means of imagining society as a kind of bodily or organic structure but also as one subject to dynamic processes of change and transformation. Like Spencer, Durkheim imagined a series of stages of social development from 'the horde' and 'the clan' through subsequent stages to 'industrial society', characterized by a process of increasing complexity in the division of labour, and consequent shifts in the manner that individuals related both to one another and the social structure (2014: 138–50). This process, according to Durkheim, was determined by 'the same law that governs biological development' (2014: 149; 2013: 167) and it applied also to the evolution of religion from immersion in the emotional effervescence of ritual in the horde, to the affective individualism of modern society (Fish 2002). From the 'protoplasm' (Durkheim 2014: 138) of proto-groups to references to 'the rings of annelida worms' (2014: 139), 'organs' (2014: 143) and 'embryonic development' (2014: 149), biology furnished Durkheim with both a means of imagining 'social evolution' (2014: 148) and for legitimizing leaps of speculative sociological thought by seeming to ground them in the apparently indisputable facts of biology and evolution.

The key inference drawn by Spencer and Durkheim from their exposure to and engagement with nineteenth-century discourses on biological evolution was the tendency in nature for simple, homogeneous structures to be surpassed by complex, heterogeneous structures. But although this was one account of evolution it was not the Darwinian one which treated 'evolution as a process of divergence', but rather it was a Lamarckian one with a 'strong emphasis on linear progress' (Bowler 2009: 87). Jean-Baptiste Lamarck had argued that evolution – or what he termed 'transformism' – offered 'the clearest evidence that creatures of every kind were working their ways up the scale of nature, with each generation taking up the cumulative achievements of its predecessors and passing them on enhanced by its own' (Ingold 2007b: 113; see also Ingold 1986: 130–1). Perhaps the clearest evidence of Lamarck's influence on the nineteenth-century study of religion can be found in Tylor's theory of 'survivals'.

Tylor defined the survival in *Primitive Culture* as 'processes, customs, opinions ... which have been carried on by force of habit into a new state of society different from that in which they had their original home' that thus 'remain as proofs and examples of an older condition of culture out of which a newer has been evolved' (Tylor 1903: I.16), while in *Anthropology: An Introduction to the Study of Man and Civilization* he described it as the 'unchanged relic of primitive man' (1881: 18). In the essay 'On the Limits of Savage Religion' (1892), Tylor had considered the problem of the 'blending of religions' (1892: 298) and the importance, as he saw it, of separating out the 'genuine ... native theology' (1892: 283) from 'accretions and transformations' (1892: 298) brought about through contact with 'civilized foreigners' (1892: 299). 'Blending' threatened Tylor's theoretical operations: his comparative anthropology enabled the postulation of origins and the reconstruction of linear sequences of beliefs and practices but required clean, unambiguous data sets. The survival was constitutive of this theoretical apparatus and he put it to use in much the same way as a geologist interpreted strata – indeed, Tylor claimed that geology established 'a principle which lies at the very foundation of the science of anthropology' (1881: 33) – or as a palaeontologist read fossils, that is, by reconstructing 'the sequence of forms *within* a line of descent' (Ingold 1986: 32; see also Marett 1936: 26; Burrow 1968: 240–1; Stocking 1995: 6). This Lamarckian rather than Darwinian vision of evolution suggested a process of continuous development whereby new traits and characteristics replaced old ones that had proven redundant in a single and unbroken line of progressive improvement (see also Opler 1964: 142–3). Tylor simply transferred Lamarck's evolutionary hypothesis across from biology to the study of culture:

> In taking up the problem of the development of culture as a branch of ethnological research, a first proceeding is to obtain a means of measurement. Seeking something like a definite line along which to reckon progression and retrogression in civilisation, we may apparently find it best in the classification of real tribes and nations, past and present. Civilisation actually existing among mankind in different grades, we are enabled to estimate and compare it by positive examples. The educated world of Europe and America practically settles a standard by simply placing its own nations at one end of the social series and savage tribes at the other, arranging the rest of mankind between these limits according as they correspond more closely to savage or to cultured life. (Tylor 1903: I.26; see also 1881: 24–5)

Tylor was far from alone in subscribing to these views: it was the paradigm of the day (albeit not uncontested) and it influenced the scholarship of Marx and Freud as well as a host of now lesser known thinkers such as John Lubbock, Henry Sumner Maine and Lewis Henry Morgan (see Kippenberg 1998: 298–300). For example, Lubbock, in *The Origin of Civilisation* (1870), suggested that

> In the first place, the condition and habits of existing savages resemble in many ways, though not in all, those of our own ancestors in a period now long gone by; in the second, they illustrate much of what is passing among

ourselves, many customs which have evidently no relation to present circumstances, and even some ideas which are rooted in our minds, as fossils are imbedded in the soil; and thirdly, we can even, by means of them, penetrate some of that mist which separates the present from the future. (1870: 1)

Tylor, then, applied the idea of a single line of progress to religion. The line was plotted from animism to science and was discernible through the study of beliefs. Tylor suggested that 'spirits are simply personified causes' (1903: II.108), a claim that set up the animistic belief in spirits as an hypothesis or explanation about the world, albeit a mistaken one. The assumption that the origins of religion lay in efforts to explain the world assumed religion was a stuttering kind of science or, in Stocking's memorable phrase, 'primitive man, in an attempt to create science, had accidentally created religion instead, and mankind had spent the rest of evolutionary time trying to rectify the error' (1987: 192). Religion was just a chapter in the story of Reason, and humanity would soon outgrow it: indeed, in the Preface to the second edition of *The Golden Bough* (1900), Frazer felt able to write:

The comparative study of the beliefs and institutions of mankind is fitted to be much more than a means of satisfying an enlightened curiosity and of furnishing materials for the researches of the learned. Well handled, it may become a powerful instrument to expedite progress ... if it shows that much which we are wont to regard as solid rests on the sands of superstition rather than on the rock of nature. It is indeed a melancholy and in some respects thankless task to strike at the foundations of beliefs in which, as in a strong tower, the hopes and aspirations of humanity through long ages have sought a refuge from the storm and stress of life. Yet sooner or later it is inevitable that the battery of the comparative method should breach these venerable walls, mantled over with ivy and mosses and wild flowers of a thousand tender and sacred associations. At present we are only dragging the guns into position: they have hardly yet begun to speak. (Frazer 1900: xxi–xxii)

In this extraordinary passage Frazer begins by opposing knowledge that 'rests on the sands of superstition', and knowledge that is built 'on the rock of nature'. The former, 'mantled over with ivy and mosses and wild flowers of a thousand tender and sacred associations' has the quality of a dream or a flight of fancy, while the latter is, by implication, solid, substantial and true. However, this truth is, in the same moment, destabilized and unhinged through the allusions to warfare ('battery' and 'guns'). Here, truth can only ultimately legitimate itself through recourse to violence. Tylor had been equally blunt. At the end of *Primitive Culture* (1903) he described anthropology as 'a reformer's science' (1903: II.453). The task? To 'expose the remains of crude old culture which have passed into harmful superstition, and to mark these out for destruction' (1903: II.453).

This violent conception of progress nevertheless assumed the existence of common human, cognitive dispositions: for example, regardless of how individuals might be separated in time and space, the ways in which they addressed problems were, according to Frazer and Tylor, predictable according to shared psychological architectures and problem-solving repertoires. It was precisely these claims about cognition and human nature that allowed them to imaginatively reconstruct apparently ancient chains of reasoning:

The intellectualist arguments of the British anthropologists took for granted certain notions of the association of ideas and the inevitable chains of causality, and they assumed that from these premises they could retrace the mental routes by which primitives had been led 'naturally' to certain beliefs and certain practices. (Needham 1972: 181)

According to Frazer, the 'comparative study of the mind of man' was 'analogous to the comparative study of his body ... undertaken by anatomy and physiology' (1931: 240): Frazer assumed that the human mind – like the human body – was structured and that its structure, origin and evolution could be explained through scientific analysis.

It is precisely this interest in the mind, and the search for specific features of religious thought, that links the Lamarckian imaginary of evolution of the late nineteenth and early twentieth centuries, to contemporary evolutionary psychology, new atheism and cognitivism (Guthrie 2013; Jong 2017). It also suggests a methodological principle that is shared by contemporary evolutionary psychologists, cognitive anthropologists and new atheists as well as Tylor, namely, that culture is not to be apprehended holistically but rather in terms of discrete units such as beliefs that can then be compared cross-culturally (see Lévi-Strauss 1993a: 4):

The bow and arrow is a species, the habit of flattening children's skulls is a species, the practice of reckoning numbers by tens is a species. The geographical distribution of these things, and their transmission from region to region, have to be studied as the naturalist studies the geography of his botanical and zoological species. (Tylor 1903: I.8)

The functionalist paradigm was founded upon extended fieldwork and was inaugurated in British anthropology by Bronislaw Malinowski (1922; but see Thornton 1985). It insisted on the study of cultures and societies as wholes that constituted their own explanatory horizon. As such, it constituted a rejection of Tylor's methods, and the hierarchies of biological evolutionism that accompanied them. Yet, like Tylor, the new cognitive approaches to religion overwhelmingly assume that religion is a by-product, but this time not of the stumbling forays and mistakes of speculative reason, but of the architecture of the mind. These approaches suppose that the human mind is not the blank slate or the black box assumed by behaviourists and social constructivists, but is instead one that comes pre-equipped with a range of biases and dispositions that are independent of and indeed precede its immersion in society and culture (Barrett 2011: 231; Boyer 2003: 123; Jong 2017: 51–2). Importantly, these biases and dispositions both enable the formation of religious beliefs and concepts but also place determinable constraints upon them. For example, the mind generates hard-wired ontological (and eminently Kantian) expectations about 'causality and motion, physical and biological objects, agency and psychology' (Jong 2017: 51). That is to say, it has expectations about cause and effect and about the behaviour of different classes of things in the world such as animals, vegetables and minerals. It also possesses theory of mind, namely, the propensity to make 'inferences about others' mental states' (Jong 2017: 57). Sperber, Boyer and others further argue that cognitive systems are organized in modular fashion, with each module tasked with specific functions, as against the idea of the mind as an all-purpose, general information processor (Boyer 1992: 43; Edwards 2003: 286). Sperber defines a module as 'a genetically specified computational device in the mind/brain' which processes 'its own inputs pertaining to some specific cognitive domain and provided by other parts of the nervous systems (e.g. sensory receptors or other modules)' (Sperber 1996: 120). Religious concepts and beliefs are notable to the extent that they contravene the basic sets of expectations delivered by these modules, but this means that there are limits on the types of religious beliefs and concepts that are likely to be transmitted and thereby spread in any given human population:

Supernatural beings are not just impossible in nature. They blatantly violate the kind of basic expectations that are delivered by domain-specific cognitive mechanisms. In direct clash with naïve physics, some are able to be in several places at the same time or to pass through solid objects.

In direct clash with naïve biology, some belong to several species at the same time or can change from one species to another. In direct clash with naïve psychology, some can literally see all past and future events ... As argued by Boyer, it is this combination of a few striking violations with otherwise conformity to ordinary expectations that makes supernatural beings attention arresting and memorable, and rich in inferential potential. (Sperber and Hirschfeld 2004: 44)

Firstly, then, religious beliefs and concepts violate the basic expectations humans have about reality, but they only violate those expectations in certain limited ways: for example, a ghost is like a person right up until the moment that it walks through a wall; a griffin is like an animal, a lion in fact, right up until the moment that it spreads its wings; a god is person-like except that it sees, hears and knows so much more than any ordinary person can (Atran and Henrich 2010: 20). Secondly, then, the memorability of religious beliefs and concepts rests on their ability to excite the mind through such contraventions, and the successful transmission of religious concepts and beliefs is understood to be dependent on these factors. According to Boyer,

First, not all products of human imagination are equally fit for widespread transmission ... in most human groups supernatural notions ... tend to centre around a small catalogue with recurrent features. This is because human minds are equipped with an *intuitive ontology*, a set of expectations about the kinds of things to be found in the world. Among the indefinitely many concepts individuals can imagine and combine, some connect with this ontology in a particular way. As a result, they stand better chances of spreading in a relatively preserved form. Second, not all culturally fit supernatural concepts are of equal social importance. Some of them are connected to representations of group identity, ritual, morality and social interaction, corresponding to what we usually call 'religion', while others are not. This difference stems from another set of cognitive capacities. Humans are greatly dependent upon cooperation and information about potential cooperators, which creates specific cognitive problems. Humans have a set of *strategic capacities* that handle these problems. Now some supernatural concepts are represented in such a way that they activate strategic capacities. As a result, they are more likely than others to generate high commitment and other psychological and social effects typical of 'religion'. (Boyer 2000: 196; italics in original)

One of the consequences of this line of thinking is the extent to which religious beliefs and religious concepts come to accrue a reproductive agency all of their own, at the expense of their human carriers. As Bering points out, 'Boyer's model holds that religious concepts gain entrance to ... mundane cognitive mechanisms through their attention-grabbing properties', going on to note that religious concepts are able 'to "parasitize" mundane cognitive mechanisms' by 'pirating aspects of human cognition' (Bering 2003: 117). This position is also the paradoxical hallmark of new atheist populism, which on the one hand celebrates Enlightenment ideals of reason and the reason-endowed, rational-choice making human subject, while on the other, uses a model derived from genetics (memetics) to account for the transmission of religious beliefs and concepts in a way that elides the role the human subject might have been expected to play in acquiring beliefs, for example through learning.

Memetics – like genetics – is a theory of information transmission. Unlike genetics, however, which deals with the transmission of information stored in DNA, memetics deals with the transmission of culture and religion as information. An evolutionary, memetic approach to religion assumes that religions can be rendered as bundles of semantic data such as beliefs whose transmission, extinction, spread and persistence in human populations can be modelled in genetics terms. According to Mesoudi, Whiten and Laland, 'cultural [or in this case, religious] knowledge is stored in brains as discrete packages of semantic information, comparable to how biological information is stored in genes' (Mesoudi, Whiten and Laland 2006: 342). The next move is to approach the diffusion or the distribution of these memes, these units of religion and culture, in the same way that geneticists study the distribution of genes in a population:

> Our individual brains are each inhabited by a large number of ideas that determine our behaviour ... An idea, born in the brain of one individual, may have, in the brains of other individuals, descendants that resemble it. Ideas can be transmitted, and by being transmitted from one person to another, they may even propagate ... Culture is made up, first and foremost, of such contagious ideas ... To explain culture, then, is to explain why and how some ideas happen to be contagious. This calls for the development of a true *epidemiology of representations*. (Sperber 1996: 1; italics in original)

As such, if a meme – in this instance, the belief in God – is like a gene, one must logically assume that human beings are hosts or carriers of that belief just as they are vehicles for self-propagating genes (Dawkins 2007: 192). Daniel Dennett begins his *Breaking the Spell* (2006) from precisely this point of departure:

> You watch an ant in a meadow, laboriously climbing up a blade of grass, higher and higher until it falls, then climbs again and again, like Sisyphus rolling his rock, always striving to reach the top. Why is the ant doing this? What benefit is it seeking for itself in this strenuous and unlikely activity? Wrong question, it turns out. No biological benefit accrues to the ant. It is not trying to get a better view of the territory or seeking food or showing off to a potential mate, for instance. Its brain has been commandeered by a tiny parasite, a lancet fluke ... that needs to get itself into the stomach of a sheep or a cow in order to complete its reproductive cycle. This little brain

worm is driving the ant into position to benefit its progeny, not the ant's. This is not an isolated phenomenon. Similarly manipulative parasites infect fish, and mice, among other species. These hitchhikers cause their hosts to behave in unlikely – even suicidal – ways, all for the benefit of the guest not the host. (Dennett 2006: 3–4)

For Dennett, religion is an analogue of the parasite *Dicrocelium dendriticum* in the ant's brain: the religion-parasite insinuates itself into the human brain but not for the benefit of the human carrier or host but for its own benefit. Its reproductive fitness is at one with its determination to have itself reproduced in other human brains. Worse, this religion-parasite not only takes advantage of its human host but actually disadvantages it, because religion is not just a belief; it is, according to Dennett, a maladaptive belief. This conclusion rests on a crude cost-benefit analysis (*'cui bono?'*) that claims that the costs of religion in terms of the time and resources that must be devoted to it far outweigh any potential benefits to the host. Religion, according to Dennett, confers no evolutionary advantage to the believer.[2]

Central to Dennett's discussion of religion and memes is a distinction between good memes and bad memes. A good meme might be something like the idea of virtue. A bad meme would be something allegedly maladaptive like the religious belief in God. But, and this is the crucial point, the basis for making this distinction does not derive from memetics or evolutionary theory more generally. Evolutionary theory provides no criteria – beyond reproductive success – to make these kinds of distinctions. Given that religion – as a meme – is extremely successful in reproductive terms, the criteria for making the distinction must ultimately be a subjective one, deriving not from evolutionary science, but from elsewhere:

According to Dennett, memes are spread according to their own criteria of success; they do not need a moral defence, and if the moral defence is

just a meme, then it cannot be morally valid in any philosophical sense ...
Dennett actually faces this question, posing it himself: 'What foundation,
then, can we stand on as we struggle to keep our feet in the meme-storm
in which we are engulfed? If replicative might does not make right, what
is to be the eternal ideal relative to which "we" will judge the value of
memes?' And his answer is: 'We should note that the memes for normative
concepts – for *ought* and *good* and *truth* and *beauty* – are among the most
entrenched denizens of our minds. Among the memes that constitute us,
they play a central role. Our existence as us, as what we as thinkers are – not
as what we as organisms are – is not independent of these memes'. If we
grant this, however, why is it that religious ideas which may seem equally
entrenched denizens of many minds are potentially dangerous? ... How
come that some basic memes are beneficial to us whereas others are not?
(Albinus 2008: 33; italics in original)

For Albinus, if a meme is really like a gene there can be no moral or political
standpoint against or for religion as a meme, only the brute fact of evolutionary
success or extinction. The critique of Religion as maladaptive cannot be
sustained on the basis of evolutionary theory. It can only be sustained on the
basis of values derived presumably from ethical, philosophical or political
resources, a point which implicates memetics and new atheism – but also
cognitive and evolutionary psychological approaches – in a politics that the
appeal to the biological imagination elides.

Cognitive, evolutionary psychological and new atheist approaches to
religion have drawn legitimacy from the idea that their impetus comes from
'religion scholars wanting to "science up" the study of religion' (Barrett 2011:
230) and, more provocatively, from claims that

The social sciences are still adrift, with an enormous mass of half-digested
observations, a not inconsiderable body of empirical generalizations, and

a contradictory stew of ungrounded, middle-level theories expressed in a babel of incommensurate technical lexicons. This is accompanied by a growing malaise, so that the single largest trend is toward rejecting the scientific enterprise as it applies to humans. We suggest that this lack of progress, this 'failure to thrive', has been caused by the failure of the social sciences to explore or accept their logical connections to the rest of the body of science – that is, to causally locate their objects of study inside the larger network of scientific knowledge. (Tooby and Cosmides 1992: 23; see also Ingold 2007a; Mesoudi, Whiten and Laland 2006, 2007)

Of course, the idea that evolutionary biology is the most scientific way to explain human behaviour – religious and otherwise – is to make a very big claim indeed. To posit the biological as the deep and sovereign truth that lies behind religion, culture and society in the way that many cognitivists, evolutionary psychologists and new atheists do is, according to Maurizio Meloni (2014a; 2014b), an attempt to advance quite a narrow and reductive view of biology. To be sure, 'if the social sciences are ill, biology looks like the therapy; if sociological investigations are thin and fragmented, biological knowledge is solid and cohesive', and if the social seems to be 'an erratic, ephemeral entity, lacking firmer ground, what is required is to anchor it onto the firmer basis of evolutionary thinking and neurobiological facts' (Meloni 2014a: 733). Yet intriguingly, what Meloni calls 'post-genomic' biology challenges the view of the 'biological as what is "genetic", "innate", "prior to social", "essential", "universal", and "invariable"' (Meloni 2014a: 732) towards the idea of the biological as 'just another interactant' (Meloni 2014a: 742). In this new, post-genomic horizon, the social and the biological turn out to be increasingly porous, such that 'there is no longer biology and culture but *hybrid resources* (interactants) in a unified developmental system' (Meloni 2014b: 606; italics in original).

Meloni's developmental systems approach treats 'biological processes as radically embedded in environmental settings in which genetic factors have no privilege' (Meloni 2014b: 604), a position that has been consistently staked out by, among others, the anthropologist Tim Ingold (1995; 2001). According to Ingold, cognition 'is not the revelation of pre-existent form but the very process wherein form is generated in the first place', and as such, analysis should take as its point of departure 'the agent-in-its-environment, or what phenomenology calls "being-in-the-world", as opposed to the self-contained individual confronting a world "out there"' (Ingold 1995: 58; see also 2001: 260–1). According to Ingold, the debate about the mind and cognition proceeds from the wrong premises: there is no unchanging, pre-engineered modular cognitive architecture, no solitary self-contained mind confronting nature, and no straightforward line of causality from the mental to the social. The mind, according to Ingold, is a series of potentials activated under different conditions rather than a set form that can be discerned at work, behind the varied products of human religion, culture and history.

If the cognitivists, evolutionary psychologists and new atheists have been somewhat coy about alternative models of cognition (see Tremlett 2011a), they have been similarly reticent about the political implications of their work. The idea that a pre-specified cognitive architecture precedes the immersion of the individual in interactive environments has allowed them to formulate the following question: 'Given the biases of the human mind, what makes religion possible?' This question has considerable political consequences (see Edwards 2003: 292), and not only because its reversal – 'Given religion, what makes the mind possible?' – is so compelling (see Durkheim 1915), while its re-configuration as 'Given psychology, what makes the mind possible?' seems too troubling to pose at all. As Foucault has argued, the turn to biology – beginning in the nineteenth century with discourses on evolution and race – was always profoundly political:

Evolutionism, understood in the broad sense – or in other words, not so much Darwin's theory itself as a set, a bundle, of notions (such as: the hierarchy of species that grow from a common evolutionary tree, the struggle for existence among species, the selection that eliminates the less fit) – naturally became within a few years during the nineteenth century not simply a way of transcribing a political discourse into biological terms, and not simply a way of dressing up a political discourse in scientific clothing, but a real way of thinking about the relations between colonization, the necessity of wars, criminality, the phenomena of madness and mental illness, the history of societies with their different cases, and so on. (Foucault 2004: 256–7)

The politics of this self-declared neutral, scientific discourse about biology, the mind and religion becomes particularly acute in the work of Harvey Whitehouse. Whitehouse's approach to religion in *Arguments and Icons* (2000) rests on a series of Durkheimian questions concerning the articulation of particular religious practices and types of religious instruction or transmission, with forms of social solidarity in Papua New Guinea. Whitehouse highlights key differences between Protestant 'doctrinal' and local, 'imagistic' religious traditions, specifically between Protestant missions and the formation of new Christian communities and indigenous traditions including male initiation rites, and their 'divergent patterns of transmission and dissemination' (2000: 80) which, according to Whitehouse, are connected to different forms of social solidarity, namely, 'anonymous communities' on the one hand, and 'highly cohesive and particularistic social ties' on the other (2000: 1).

Whitehouse seeks to explain these contrasting forms of religiosity, instruction, transmission and solidarity in terms of cognitive memory systems which are hard-wired and biologically given, namely, semantic memory that 'is concerned with abstract knowledge of the world' and which is 'encoded in generalized schemas', and episodic memory which is 'concerned with actual occurrences in a person's experience, in which the time and place of encoding form part of the representation in memory' (2000: 113). According to

Whitehouse, semantic, schema-based memory forms the biological basis for Protestant doctrinal knowledge that is typically transmitted through repetitive forms of worship and study and which is in turn linked to the emergence of imagined communities of the kind described by Benedict Anderson (2016). Episodic memory, by contrast, is articulated through rites of initiation and terror (Whitehouse 2000: 21–3) that 'serve to bind together members of local religious communities, whose common revelatory experience evokes intense and lasting solidarity of a sort that cannot be verbally articulated' (2000: 112).

Whitehouse's interest in memory systems, religion and forms of social solidarity is political because he himself poses a clear and direct line of causality between evolved cognitive architectures and religio-social morphologies:

> The relevance of memory for social theory was first substantially explored by Halbwachs, whose work has recently been revisited in a spate of fresh scholarship on 'collective' and 'social' memory. By and large, this literature focuses on the ideological content of memory, and the political dynamics of repression, forgetting, selective recall, decay/distortion, and alternative discourses about memory. At the heart of many studies is the question of who controls representations of the past, and to what ends. The central thrust of my argument goes in the opposite direction. Instead of asking how political organization and ideology help to mould people's memories, I am asking whether universal features of human memory, activated in different ways, might be said to mould political organization and ideology. (Whitehouse 2000: 5; cf. Connerton 1989)

These claims are developed further in *Modes of Religiosity* (2004) where Whitehouse states that his work concerns 'the causal interconnections between a set of cognitive and socio-political features' (2004: 64), re-stating the suggestion that 'cognitive features are linked to particular social morphology' (2004: 66). The political burden of such a project is considerable, perhaps especially because of the large claims made on behalf of the cognitive approach in terms of the reliability of its data and its methods.

The biological imagination has been shaped by a project committed to defining and explaining religion and for accounting, somehow, for the popularity of beliefs that nevertheless seem to be demonstrably false. For the likes of Durkheim, Frazer, Spencer and Tylor, biological evolution functioned as a guarantee for the idea of linear, developmental, historical progress. Religion was akin to an ill-adapted organism doomed to extinction in a hostile environment and a pointless appendage or organ that would shrivel, wither and die without harm to the host. The death of religion would ultimately ensure the eventual correspondence of the contents of human minds with the real world outside. According to George Stocking,

> The Industrial Revolution may be regarded as the practical implementation of the eighteenth-century belief in human rationality, and nineteenth-century sociocultural evolutionism was a reformulation, in terms appropriate to the later British utilitarian tradition, of eighteenth-century accounts of the progress of the human mind. At every level, human beings tried to understand and control the world around themselves and adapt their behaviour to it. Progress in positive knowledge – and therefore in effective rationality – consisted in a closer coordination of the external world and internal mental representations of it, largely by the elimination of reasoning that was either erroneously founded or no longer adaptive. (Stocking 1987: 200)

More than a century later, Religion's stubborn persistence continues to demand an explanation: this time, evolutionary psychology is the guarantor of human rationality and of the potential for the correspondence of mental representations with the world as it actually is. The paradox is this: the more the evolutionists and cognitivists have tried to find a ground for the reasoning subject by pitting it against all the apparent unreasonings or anti-reasonings of Religion, the reasoning subject itself has become more and more ethereal, slipping away either as a chimera on an elusive developmentalist horizon or as an airy nothing floating among a series of hard-wired cognitive systems.

The biology offered by Deleuze and Guattari allows for the possibility not so much to escape these problems as to fundamentally change the question being asked. Interestingly, it is Deleuze and Guattari's reflections on Darwin (2014: 55) that suggest the point of departure. Darwin's focus was on populations as aggregates of characteristics, rather than on species as fixed types:

First, Darwin replaces types with populations. What this means is that Darwin does not see species as a fixed type, he sees a species as a temporary and statistical aggregate of traits. Second, Darwin replaces degrees (of difference) between species for differential relations. The issue here concerns the development from one species into another. If a species is a population, then its traits will be grouped around a more or less stable point. However, at the margins the members of a population will deviate from the mean and possess a different differential relation among traits. The classic example here is the peppered moth. Prior to the industrial revolution in England the dominant colour in the population was white with dark spots … This colour provided excellent camouflage against the light-coloured tree trunks of the time. At the margins of the population of moths, though, a few were darker. As pollution increased with the industrial revolution the tree trunks became darker. As a result, the darker moths were better camouflaged. This shift in colour became dominant in the population. Recently, a decrease in pollution in England has reversed the process again, and now light coloured moths are dominant. Deleuze and Guattari think this process is better accounted for not in terms of degrees, where we would posit a series of increasingly darker moths, but as a differential relation within the population in which the statistical aggregate of traits re-organizes into a new statistical aggregate. (Adkins 2015: 53)

Rather than assume that Religion is a type or a species with definite traits concentrated around a fixed point, why not instead imagine traits dis-aggregating and re-aggregating to generate new formations and assemblages in tune with socio-ecological shifts? Deleuze and Guattari's (2014) conceptions of the body without organs and the rhizome open up a counter-biological imaginary precisely for re-thinking religions as flows, coagulations and disintegrations.

Christianities, rhizomes and the body without organs

Deleuze and Guattari borrowed the idea of the body without organs from the French playwright, Antonin Artaud (Adkins 2015: 40). For Artaud, the body without organs was a means for thinking beyond the body as a solid or organized entity towards something capable of change. The idea of the body without organs is, then, precisely intended to shatter the idea of identity or organization: it suggests a 'disarticulated, dismantled, and deterritorialized [body] … able [nevertheless] to be reconstituted in new ways' (Best and Kellner 1991: 91). Similarly, Deleuze and Guattari's conception of the rhizome – opposed throughout A Thousand Plateaus (2014) to the tree as a metaphor of hierarchy and stasis – offers a compelling means for privileging not forms and solids, but flows and liquids:

> Rhizomes do not propagate by way of clearly delineated hierarchies but by underground stems in which any part may send additional shoots upward, downward, or laterally. There is no hierarchy. There are no clear lines of descent. A rhizome has no beginning or end. It is always in the middle … The key to the rhizome … is that the rhizome continually creates the new. It is not predictable. It does not follow a linear pattern of growth and reproduction. Its connections are lateral not hierarchical. (Adkins 2015: 23)

The rhizome works against what Deleuze and Guattari call 'arborescent systems' (2014: 16; see Best and Kellner 1991: 98–9 and Marks 1998: 45): rhizomes are flows which are not organized vertically, hierarchically or genealogically, or according to any centrally constituted coordinates, but are rather 'acentered' (2014: 22), spreading in all directions.

According to Adkins, the point of the body without organs and the rhizome is to enable a particular kind of questioning. For example, 'what are the connections that constitute this entity?' and 'what further connections are made possible and impossible by this particular set of connections?' (Adkins 2015: 9). If a 'World Religion' such as Christianity is re-envisioned in terms of the body without organs and the rhizome, what will it look like? Will Christianity be a fixed thing or a flow punctuated by temporary stabilizations of experience, practice and belief?

Andrew Walls (2010) and Diarmaid MacCulloch (2010) have both stressed the plurality of Christian traditions, its multiple geographies, histories, connectivities and translations. According to Walls,

> Christianity has existed for two millennia. During that time, its geographical and cultural centre of gravity has shifted several times. It has adapted itself to diverse societies and both shaped and been shaped by them. In some ways it has been the most syncretistic of the great faiths … The result has been successive translations in terms of different languages and cultures, and often of the sub-cultures within them. This in turn has involved a repeated process of cross-cultural transmission followed by cultural interpretation. (Walls 2010: 61)

MacCulloch replicates these two gestures, the first to the 'instability' (2010: 2) of Christianity and its 'capacity to mutate' (2010: 9), and the second – intriguingly framed in almost vitalist terms – to claim that 'the nature of tradition is not that of a humanly manufactured mechanical or architectural structure, with a constant outline and form, but rather that of a plant, pulsing with life and continually changing shape while keeping the same ultimate identity' (MacCulloch 2010: 7–8). But, both Walls and MacCulloch want to hold on to the idea of 'Christianity'. Its history might be long and complex and its edges might be blurred, but it must have a centre – an essence – that holds. According to Francisco (2018), by contrast, the 'mixing of Christianity in its particular historical mediations with other social and religious traditions … indicates that its borders are de facto porous, if not movable' (2018: 263), and, if the 'focus is on Christianity as enduring tradition, then its borders appear more delineated. With a pluralistic lens, its borders could easily be transgressed. But when Christianity is viewed as "lived religion" or with a post-tradition perspective, its borders are considered porous' (2018: 264). By contrast, the Filipino theologian Jose Mario C. Francisco experiments with the concept of hybridity as a means of envisioning evangelization in a way that transforms it from 'a unidirectional, deductive process (from faith to culture)' to a 'dynamic and multidirectional encounter' (Francisco 2018: 260) the effects of which cannot be specified in advance.

Francisco's theology, in common with much of the thrust of the anthropology of Christianity, anticipates a conception of religions and of Christianities as flows and the forms in which they appear as always temporary and always already entangled in configurations of culture, state and economy. Similarly, Fenella Cannell's question 'what, in any situation is Christianity, and how can one … discern its lineaments from that of the social context in which it lives?' (Cannell 2006: 13), demands that Christianity is taken not as a given, discrete object but rather as a process that is always under (de)construction. In a similar vein, Malory Nye has argued that rather than studying Christianity as a crystallized tradition or as a simple fact on the ground, one should examine 'the various cultural, religious, and political manifestations which have at different times been labelled as "Christianity"' and 'how these different forms of religioning are indeed different from each other, but also how through certain political discourses and practices have achieved the valuable status of legitimacy as the same "thing" (i.e. Christianity)' (Nye 2000: 467–8), or in short, the processes, sites and occasions through which Christianity is produced (and produces itself) as an object that can be disentangled from the social contexts in which it is embedded.

These kinds of questions are not idle, theoretical speculations. The emergence of different Christianities in different regions of the world, and the multiple, overlapping scales of local, national and global connections they have set in motion, bring to the fore the intellectual hazards of assuming the existence of any discrete, coherent and continuous, singular object called Christianity. As such, Francisco (2018), Cannell (2006) and Nye (2000) open the door to an approach that begins not with a fixed form but with historical, ethnographic and rhizomatic flows and coagulations. In what follows I apply these methodological ideas to a Southeast Asian Christianity.

The Flores assemblage

Flores is a small island towards the eastern end of the Indonesian archipelago with a complex history. In 1859 the Dutch concluded negotiations with the Portuguese – negotiations that had begun some eight years previously – and bought Eastern Flores and the neighbouring islands, promising to recognize the Catholic populations already established there in the island's coastal villages (Steenbrink 2003). Catholic missionary activity continued in the islands even though they were now under Dutch jurisdiction. But, with colonial policy objectives shifting, the beginning of the twentieth century saw the Dutch seeking to make the islands more profitable: they planted new export crops, imposed new taxes and built new roads to open the islands up further to the gaze of the colonial state. The period saw a concomitant increase in Catholic missionary activity in the area, with the number of missionaries rising from 52 in 1911 to 222 in 1939

(Steenbrink 2007: 81). The increased penetration of the colonial government and of Catholic missionaries to the interior of Flores and the mountainous Ngada region gathered pace from about 1910 with the building of new schools, and the villages of the region converted to Catholicism in the 1920s.

Fast-forward to the 1980s, the Indonesian New Order government regarded Ngada primarily in developmental terms, that is, as backward and isolated. However, its stunning geography including the volcano Keli Mutu with its three, different coloured crater lakes, the nearby Komodo National Park (Cole 2007: 947), and the emergence of a new kind of exotic or orientalist tourist gaze (Urry 2002) seeking out performances of ethnic and cultural identity including religious rituals and archaeological remains and artefacts to complement the staple tourist diet of beaches and scenery, provided a stimulus. The Indonesian state soon realized the economic potential of tourism for Ngada, and began to use it as a vehicle for cultivating local ethnic identity and a sense of participation in an Indonesian national imaginary (King and Wilder 2003: 221). Indeed, four Ngada villages were designated as 'national heritage' sites in the 1992 Law No. 5, which specified the Preservation of Cultural Sites and Objects (Cole 2007: 951). The law required that the villages be maintained in such a way that they retained their 'traditional' character. Michel Picard's observation that, 'far from being an external force striking a local society from without, tourism – or, rather ... the touristification of a society – proceeds from within' (Picard 1997: 183), usefully highlights local sites of agency in preparing certain sights, objects and performances to be seen in a certain way and the potential for tourist revenue to revitalize and empower a local community. At the same time, however, the law made real the prospect that the villagers would be denied the benefits of Indonesian modernity – for example, electricity – on the grounds that it might spoil the primitive authenticity of the villages (Cole 2007: 952).

Ngada villages consist of 'wooden houses with high thatched roofs ... arranged in two parallel lines or around the sides of a rectangle' (Cole 2007: 948). In the centre are carved wooden representations of the male and female clan ancestors and standing stones, or megaliths. Importantly, there is a significant dissonance in the way the megaliths are understood by villagers, the Indonesian tourist board and by the tourists who come to visit. For the villagers the megaliths are living things that signify the ancestors and relations between the living and the dead, and are essential to ongoing ritual relations between the living and the dead that require ritual animal sacrifice as regulated by *adat* or customary law. However, for both the Indonesian tourist board and the tourists – albeit for different reasons – they signify an ancient and pagan past. For the tourists the idea that the villagers might be Catholics and ancestor worshippers at the same time, is perhaps particularly troubling:

> Tourists are faced with cultural confusion: the megaliths in the hamlets are found alongside Catholic graves with cement headstones and wooden crosses. To the casual observer megaliths are part of a culture that was a relic of the villagers' past; if the villagers are now Catholics then the megaliths belong to past beliefs ... Following the guidebooks, many tourists visit an old village site where they just gaze upon megaliths ... Tourists sometimes use local children to find the site and these children frequently climb and play on the stones. Tourists often equate this with children showing a disregard for the megaliths and therefore conclude that these relics have no contemporary importance for the villagers. (Cole 2003: 147–8)

Cole's description of some of the confusions occasioned by the Flores assemblage demonstrates the entanglement of Ngada Catholicism with tourism and nationalism and the plurality of simultaneous religious and cultural identifications, specifically Catholicism, *adat* and traditional religion. Pulling at just one of the elements of the assemblage does not enable their separation but rather shows off their complex entanglement and co-integration. As the Catholic theologian and historian Karel Steenbrink has noted with respect to Catholicism in Indonesia,

The (often partial) acceptance of the new faith by indigenous people did not always involve the (partial or total) rejection of older traditions. The idea of exclusive religious doctrines and practices is uncommon in most tribal religions, as is that of exclusive adherence to a separate set of rituals, doctrines, and ethical precepts, known as religion. Most traditional societies also have independent systems for rituals, attached to the social and political system, for the practice of individual healers and magicians. To this already complex religious system a new entity was added, a universal religion, with its centre outside the traditional area in time and space. In matters of marriage and contacts with the dead, the influence of the new religion remained very weak. It was, however, very successful in aspects of life related to modernity, [such as the] education of children in schools and health care. (Steenbrink 2003: 234)

Does this one example from a small Indonesian island represent anything more generalized or is it an exotic outlier? If the former, it might be something along the following lines: religions are flows, always on the move, taking new and different forms in different times and places. Flores Christianity belongs less to a continuous global tradition or for that matter to a definite phenomenon delimited in scholarship by the term 'Religion', but is rather just one temporary coagulation of Christianity. As Benson Saler has argued, the 'phenomena commonly comprehended by applications of the word "religion" are too complex and variable, and often too enmeshed with other phenomena in a larger universe, to be confined analytically within sharp, impermeable boundaries' (Saler 2000: 196). Perhaps, then, religions are productively conceived of as rhizomes or as bodies without organs, that is, as a-centred assemblages of elements best approached not as static objects characterized by fixed traits but as flows of shifting repertoires.

3

Generative Interactivity

Introduction

How do religions and societies change? Eighteenth- and nineteenth-century theories of change were concerned with uncovering laws and regularities according to which natural and social forms evolved. In the anthropology of religion, E. B. Tylor proposed the evolution of religion from a few simple, animist beliefs developing through a fixed, linear sequence of stages to monotheism, before culminating in science. In political economy, Adam Smith imagined simple systems of barter and exchange as the logical precursors of transactions conducted using money and underwritten by a legal framework enforced by the state, a handy just-so story that explained and legitimated both the emergence of capitalism and private property (Graeber 2014b: 24–8). Likewise in sociology, Herbert Spencer argued that the direction of social change could be inferred from the laws of biological evolution, which he took to indicate a series of transformations in the direction of increasing complexity (Spencer 1972). In each case, change was conceived as a teleological transformation from simple, flexible, improvised or liquid forms into more formal, solid, institutionalized and organized ones.

Twentieth-century theories of change focused on the West's modernity, but the starting point was less the formation of solid, dependable forms than the dangers of their disintegration. Modernity was conceptualized as progress and as the freeing of reason from tradition and religion. The redundancy and inevitable liquefaction of religion was taken for granted, and the secularization thesis was the product of these assumptions. However, there was a second take on modernity, a version inflected with romanticism and vitalism, a version that articulated a critique of reason, rationalism and objectivism, and which lamented the loss of shared, inter-subjectively held meanings and values thought to reside in religion and the 'life-world'.

The spelling out of this alternative discourse on modernity was the project of critical theory: to offer, amidst modernity's turbulence, a critique of capitalism and accompanying processes of rationalization, a critique that would try to ensure that the vital energies of the life-world were insulated from destruction by the instrumental logics of capital and reason. This critique is implicated in the lived religion thesis. Christopher Partridge's two-volume *The Re-Enchantment of the West* (2004) and Paul Heelas's *Spiritualities of Life* (2008) are examples of an approach in the study of religions positioned, as it were, to the side – or is that the left? – of the secularizationists, which claims that the new, extra- and post-institutional forms of religion in the West are responses to the reductionisms of modernity, with the new religions cast as the unlikely saviours of the Habermasian life-world. According to Partridge, the 'secularizing forces of rationalization, bureaucratization and technological domination' (Partridge 2004: 43) have been unable to complete their domination of the social, leaving a space for a return 'to a form of magical culture' he terms 'occulture' (2004: 40). According to Partridge, 'occulture' is a reservoir of practices, symbols and ideas that privilege notions of the archaic, the authentic and the primitive. Making similar moves, Heelas foregrounds what he calls 'inner-life' and 'experiential spirituality' (Heelas 2008: 5, 219), arguing that they lie on a 'romantic trajectory' running counter to a modernity that is 'ever more regulated by legal, quasi-legal or economically justified procedures, rules, [and] systems' (2008: 2). For Partridge and for Heelas, it is precisely the improvised spaces of the new religions and spiritualities that promise liberation from a suffocating and totalitarian modernity.

And yet these Cold War deliberations seem increasingly adrift from the world of the early twenty-first century. Max Weber's brooding thesis on the emergence of capitalism, the capitalism of Taylorism and Fordism but also of piety and religious striving mediated by a salvation anxiety precipitated by feelings of 'unprecedented loneliness' (Weber 2002: 60), is dead, and the state – at least in the disciplinary form imagined by Foucault (1991) and others – seems likewise to be undergoing a process of radical reconfiguration. In their stead, something darker and more dangerous has appeared. Capitalism is no longer an 'iron cage' (Weber 2002: 123) built on an edifice of austere, machine-body discipline but, according to George González, a new capitalism has emerged that engages the sensualities of the body in endless consumption, a new 'cybernetic' (2015: 111) and 'fast' (2015: 167) capitalism that he describes in terms of 'disruptive energies' (González 2015: 74). González's capitalism echoes that of Zygmunt Bauman (2000) and David Harvey (1990) except that he adds to the mix the trope of the demonic (2015: 110–16). If liquid religion seemed to promise a kind of liberation from the disciplinary aspects of modern society, liquid capitalism threatens to swallow everything in a storm of unparalleled magnitude.

Amidst these concerns with liquids, solids, progress and demonic change, stands functionalism. The functionalist approach to social structure and morphology treated societies as 'homogeneous, organised and self-reproducing' wholes (Bloch 1977: 279). E. E. Evans-Pritchard's discussion of Nuer society captured this sense of social structure as something that endured apparently impervious to the kinds of forces alluded to above, in the following terms:

By social structure we mean relations between groups which have a high degree of consistency and constancy. The groups remain the same irrespective of their specific content of individuals at any particular moment, so that generation after generation of people pass through them. Men are born into them, or enter into them later in life, and move out of them at death; the structure endures. (Evans-Pritchard 1940: 262)

In these pages, change is conceived in terms of generative interaction. As briefly and succinctly as possible, the teleologies of modernity are rejected. Change is not pre-ordained to follow a particular script or direction. The agencies of change are complex and certainly exceed the human. However, change is not demonic. It is discernible and discoverable and it begins with an insistence on the primacy of flow and the transiency of the fixed or solid: that is, solid, static forms or morphologies are not eternal but are rather temporary stabilizations or coagulations of elements on their way to a transformation into something new. The point is to attend to the moments at which these temporary coagulations form and break down. In his ground-breaking ethnography *Political Systems of Highland Burma* (2004) Edmund Leach developed an oscillation model of social structure that described how Kachin/Shan social groups shimmered between *gumsa* (horizontal, anarchistic) and *gumlao* (vertical, autocratic) structural morphologies. It anticipates the approach I take here, and as a rejection of functionalist holism it is worth quoting in full:

A study of Kachin social organisation cannot ... proceed in the classical manner which treated culture groups as social isolates. This classical manner in ethnography may be summarised thus: It is assumed that within a somewhat arbitrary geographical area a social system exists; the population involved in this social system is of one culture; the social system is uniform. Hence the anthropologist can choose for himself a locality 'of any convenient size' and examine in detail what goes on in this locality; from this examination he will hope to reach conclusions about the principles of organisation operating in this particular locality ... It is quite clear that in the Kachin case, generalisation of this kind would be invalid. The social system is not uniform ... I assume that within a somewhat arbitrarily defined area – namely the Kachin Hills Area – a social system exists. The valleys between the hills are included in this area so that Shan and Kachin are, at this level, part of a single social system. Within this major social system there are, at any given time, a number of significantly different sub-systems which are inter-dependent ... Considered simply as patterns of organisation these sub-systems may be thought of as variations on a theme ... any such equilibrium as may appear to exist may in fact be of a very transient and unstable kind. (2004: 60–1)

Leach proposed a dynamic, empirical account of Kachin/Shan reality, one in which forms and flows were conceived as undergoing constant processes of coagulation and dissolution, that is, one in which forms could be apprehended as in a constant process of oscillation between centripetal forces of structuring and centrifugal forces of disintegration.

Given the primacy given to flows and liquids by scholars interested in lived religion, perhaps the likes of Nancy Ammerman (2007), Edward Bailey (1998), Kees de Groot (2006; 2008), Graham Harvey (2013), Meredith McGuire (2008) and Leonard Primiano (1995) (among others), in their advocacy of the study of the improvised micro-practices of ordinary life through which religions are lived out not by individuals ventriloquizing doctrines but by ordinary people building religious lives from the *bric-à-brac* of whatever comes to hand, are ahead of the curve. The lived religion thesis certainly owes something to earlier conceptions of 'popular' religion and the 'little' tradition even though those terms were always, in some vague, unspecified sense, referents to inauthentic, adulterated forms of religion that the virtuosi would purify if they could (see Orsi 2002: xiii–xix). But these models of religion did draw attention to the fact that actual religious lives are hardly lived out in accordance with doctrinal or official precepts (Schielke and Debevec 2012: 1–8). Importantly, the turn to what has been variously termed 'liquid religion', 'lived religion', 'implicit religion' and 'vernacular religion' constitutes a certain celebration of religions as flows of ever-changing combinations of elements, assembled together by creative individuals in the biographical streams of their lives. It marks a considerable departure from the quantitative sociology of the likes of Steve Bruce and David Voas and their implicit assumption that, when it comes to religions, only the solid is significant. For Bruce and Voas, the fact of secularization – the fact of the successive, generational thinning out of institutional, religious populations particularly in the national churches of northwestern Europe – points unambiguously to the conclusion that religious institutions will soon experience a level of population density so low that institutional transmission and reproduction will soon be impossible. On the one hand, then, there is the lived religion hypothesis which proposes a permanent state of religious liquidity or becoming that is implicated in the biographies of individuals to such an exquisite degree of minuteness, that processes of coagulation or calcification never occur. This, however, is not a realistic position. On the other hand, there is the secularization thesis which discounts the significance of liquidity altogether, and weds itself solely to the analysis of institutional solids and their disintegration. This is also an unrealistic position and neither is it mitigated much by Stark and Bainbridge's oscillation model of secularization (Stark and Bainbridge 1987).

The objective of this chapter is to offer a radically different account of religious and social change and, as such, I trace three steps: in the first I address the work of Karl Marx and, in particular, his attempt to model processes of social change. In the second, I turn to the work of Claude Lévi-Strauss and the structuralist model of myths and their transformation. Both of these models anticipate change according to certain interactions of elements, interactions that occur without, necessarily, the agency of any subject. In the third and most substantial part of this chapter, I flesh out a set of four Christo-Filipino assemblages. Each assemblage is constituted spatially and each appears to be a transformation of the others. They do not play into any fable of progress or sorry tale of entropic despair. They avoid the methodological errors made by proponents of liquid, lived and vernacular religion, which are consistently marked by the positing of the meaning- and rational-choice making individual as the unit of analysis and as the agent of change. Here, instead, change is the property of the assemblage and of the energy of its human and non-human elements and their interactions. The privileging of the assemblage also side-steps the methodological mistakes made by supporters of the secularization thesis for which religious and social change occurs according to a doubtful teleology of religious deconsolidation, and which depends on the idea of the individual as a unitary entity where belief and action are in perfect harmony. The assemblage, indeed, allows for a precise plotting of the transition or tipping points between solid and liquid forms – when one assemblage transforms and generates new versions of itself.

Marx and change

Marxism encompasses less a single tradition or body of theory than intersecting strands of Leninist, Trotskyist, Gramscian, critical, neo- and post-Marxist interpretations and legacies. I am interested in the 'Marxism without guarantees' of the kind proposed by Stuart Hall (Hall 1983) and the sophisticated, post-structuralist inflected re-thinking of key aspects of Marx's work – notably his ideas about history and ideology – by Chantal Mouffe and Ernesto Laclau (Laclau and Mouffe 1985; Laclau 1990). For example, in *New Reflections on the Revolution of Our Time* (1990), Laclau contrasts Marx's descriptions of social and historical change in *The Communist Manifesto*, with that in the Preface to *A Critique of Political Economy*. Laclau argues that in the *Manifesto* Marx privileges society as a site of struggle, suggesting that the social is never closed but is always open to the possibility of change. Importantly, this is 'not as the result of the empirical impossibility of its specific coherence being fulfilled, but as something which "works" within the structure from the beginning' (Laclau 1990: 29). Like a Derridean text under deconstruction, the Laclau-Marxist historically contingent social formation is always already prey to forces of change by ripples and perturbations and the possibility that the 'slight movement produces a revolution out of nothing' (Derrida 1997: 257).

In the Preface, by contrast, Marx frames social change in terms of a pair of closed, pre-determined levels of analysis – that is, base and superstructure – and in terms of the specification of a limited set of primary and secondary linear relations of cause and effect:

> In the social production of their life, men enter into definite relations that are indispensable and independent of their will, relations of production which correspond to a definite stage of development of their material productive forces. The sum total of these relations of production constitutes the economic structure of society, the real foundation, on which arises a legal and political superstructure and to which correspond definite forms of social consciousness. The mode of production of material life conditions the social, political and intellectual life process in general. It is not the consciousness of men that determines their being, but, on the contrary, their social being that determines their consciousness. At a certain stage of their development, the material productive forces of society come in conflict with the existing relations of production or – what is but a legal expression for the same thing – with the property relations within which they have been at work hitherto. From forms of development of the productive forces these relations turn into their fetters. Then begins an epoch of social revolution. With the change of the economic foundations the entire immense superstructure is more or less rapidly transformed. In considering such transformations a distinction should always be made between the material transformation of the economic conditions of production, which

can be determined with the precision of natural science, and the legal, political, religious, artistic or philosophic – in short, ideological forms in which men become conscious of this conflict and fight it out. (Marx [in McLellan] 1995: 163)

The passage can be broken down into its constitutive elements which can be summarized as follows: (i) people are born into pre-existing relationships or what Marx calls 'relations of production' (namely, the dominant social relationships through which a society is able to transmit its values and reproduce itself through time) and these (ii) correspond with a 'stage' in the 'development of their material forces of production' (the word 'stage' is indicative of a certain, evolutionist conception of history while the 'material forces of production' refer to the kinds of technology available in the work of social reproduction); (iii) taken as a whole, the relations of production and the material forces of production form the 'economic structure' or 'real foundation' and upon this foundation arises a 'superstructure' of 'social', 'political' and 'intellectual' forms. Importantly, social existence 'determines' consciousness, that is, it determines both the what and how of thought; (iv) 'at a certain stage of development' conflict occurs between the forces of production and the relations of production, leading to a period of 'social revolution' and the transformation first of the economic base of society and then the superstructure; (v) the study of periods of rapid social change should distinguish between the 'material transformation' of the economic base of society which can be 'determined with the precision of a natural science', and the 'ideological forms in which men become conscious of this conflict and fight it out', phrasing that suggests a radical discontinuity between ordinary or everyday experience of a period of rapid social change and the kind of knowledge of such a period that can be delivered by scientific study, a break that corresponds with the delineation of 'ideological' or ordinary forms of knowledge on the one hand, and scientific or objective forms on the other.

In the Preface, Marx's use of the idea of ideology presupposes the existence of an outside to society and history from which judgements can be made as to the truth or falsity of particular accounts and narrations of social change. It is precisely this Marxist incarnation of the Enlightenment knowing subject that Laclau undermines. By contrast, the insistence on seeing the social as a terrain of struggle, and on knowledge as produced amidst those struggles, means that the concept of ideology can acquire a different weight: rather than a means of measuring truth it can instead indicate the problem of the opacity of the social to enquiry – and perhaps the capacity of contingent social and religious elements to interact and generate unexpected social forms. However, the inevitable result of this move is to remove the privileged perspective on the social that Marxism once claimed to offer.

Structuralism, myth and transformation

Distributed at the intersections of sociology, philosophy, anthropology, psychoanalysis, linguistics, folklore, history and political science (but also, and probably more importantly, cybernetics, mathematics, biology, art and music), structuralism and post-structuralism have conventionally been associated with a turn to language in social theory (Callinicos 1999: 266) and with a rejection of humanism including the death of the author (Barthes 1977: 148) and the erasure of 'Man' (Lévi-Strauss 1966: 247; Foucault 1970: 387). Indeed, structuralism and post-structuralism were distilled, according to sceptical Anglo-Saxon commentators, in a Parisian laboratory somewhere on the left bank from the work of a Swiss linguist whose key book seemed to suggest that the meaningfulness of words resided in language rather than the intentions of any putative speaker (which was ironic given that it was composed, after his death, from the notes taken by his students during his lectures), and a Viennese doctor who was convinced that the dreams and verbal slips of his bourgeois patients did not mean what they appeared to mean on the surface. There was also the work of a German philologist – work that was comprehensively ignored until long after his death in the mad house. That structuralism and post-structuralism are purported to have exposed the illusion of meaning's guarantee under the fiduciary signs of the author, Man, and God, bears all the hallmarks of that German's furious tirade against metaphysics.

Yet structuralism and post-structuralism are more than exquisite deliberations on language. Beyond the writings of Ferdinand de Saussure, Sigmund Freud and Friedrich Nietzsche, the structuralist approach which convulsed anthropology and the study of religions in the 1960s and 1970s was very much an intervention in debates initiated by evolutionist thinkers such as James G. Frazer on totemism (1910) and functionalist thinkers such as Bronislaw Malinowski on myth (1984). Within Frazer's evolutionist framework, totemism evolved into religion and religion into science. Societies were ordained to progress – implicitly either under Western tutelage or according to parameters established according to the Western experience of modernity – stage by stage, away from religion and towards science, industry and property-owning democracy in a journey towards civilization. This linear theory of historical transformation was challenged by structuralism and later post-structuralism, which posed a series of non-linear models whereby change occurred not as the result of any theory of progress but according to contingent and complex interactions of elements. According to Malinowski's functionalist framework, myths functioned homeo-statically to sustain social order in primitive societies serving 'principally to establish a sociological charter' (Malinowski 1984: 144). However, re-framed according to structuralist and post-structuralist logics, myths and societies were transformed into complex forms subject not to functionalist laws of closed-system equilibrium but to open-system dynamics and non-linear processes of transformation.

It is worth noting that the linguistic turn also inspired an interpretive and humanist anthropology conceived very much in opposition to structuralism.

Clifford Geertz took issue with anthropological analyses 'based on formal verification, replicability, [and] prediction' (Silverman 1990: 131; see also Geertz 1973: 29), claiming that the study of culture was 'not an experimental science in search of law, but an interpretive one in search of meaning' (Geertz 1973: 5). Geertz embraced phenomenological interpretivism inspired by his readings of Max Weber and Paul Ricoeur and, borrowing the notion of 'thick description' from Gilbert Ryle, he argued that the business of anthropology was meaning as a product of human intention.

Geertz's interpretive, cultural anthropology drew its intellectual nourishment from the hermeneutic tradition of Western philosophy. If, in the interpretation of a text, the hermeneut moved from word to sentence and from text to context to establish textual meaning, so Geertz the ethnographer moved in 'fields of synecdoches' (Clifford 1983: 131) from action to cultural whole:

> What the ethnographer is in fact faced with ... is a multiplicity of complex conceptual structures, many of them superimposed upon or knotted into one another, which are at once strange, irregular, and inexplicit, and which he must contrive somehow first to grasp and then to render ... Doing ethnography is like trying to read (in the sense of 'construct a reading of') a manuscript – foreign, faded, full of ellipses, incoherencies, suspicious emendations, and tendentious commentaries, but written not in conventionalised graphs of sound but in transient examples of shaped behaviour. (Geertz 1973: 10)

According to Geertz, to see culture as something readable altered the 'sense of what ... interpretation is', shifting it toward 'modes of thought rather more familiar to the translator, the exegete, or the iconographer than to the test giver' (Geertz 1983: 31). But Geertz privileged not the unstable dialogism of Bakhtin or the deconstruction of Derrida. Rather, drawing from Ricoeur (ibid.), 'Geertz's texts do not engender multiple, typically ambiguous or conflicting readings. They seem to reach unitary solutions' (Silverman 1990: 128). Geertz privileged meaning but it was meaning in the singular – clear, unified and untroubled. As such, Geertz's formulation of culture-as-text imagined anthropological research as an attempt to render 'the unruly meanings of a text in a single, coherent intention' (Clifford 1983: 132), except that this intention did not refer to a single author as it would have done had the text been, for example, a (Western) novel, but rather a generalized author such as 'the Balinese', with Geertz cast in the role as the master arbiter of 'what the Balinese mean'.

By contrast, structuralism denied the centrality of intentional meaning, substituting it with a focus not on speakers as meaning-makers but on speakers as subjects of systems. As such, it has been characterized as a mode of analysis that privileges structures (or structuring structures) said to function like grammar in language – that is, like an unconscious set of rules that determine sequences of words although these rules remain largely hidden to ordinary language speakers. An opposition of grammar (*langue*) to speech (*parole*) and of a hidden depth to a visible surface was a key feature of Saussure's linguistics. Saussure developed a series of further oppositions – diachronic to synchronic, signifier to signified, and syntagmatic to paradigmatic – to capture a sense of language as a system of (ordinarily hidden) rules and relationships, for which the focus of analysis was not individual (speakers of) words as carriers of meaning but the structuring relations between words. Frederic Jameson has described this as a 'movement from a substantive way of thinking to a relational one' (Jameson 1972: 13).

For Saussure, the structural study of language concentrated not on speech as it unfolded in time (diachronically) but on grammar as a system that might be caught in an analytical snap shot (synchronically). According to Saussure, language was a system of differences – acoustic differences of sound and ideational differences of meaning (for an overview see Sturrock 1993). Words (signs) signify or point, but meaning resides not in signs/words as containers of meaning – there is no essential tie between signs and that to which they refer – but is generated according to horizontal, syntagmatic relations of combination (that is, the positioning of personal pronouns in relation to verbs in a sentence) and vertical, paradigmatic relations of substitution (for example, the use of a word in a sentence always implies the potential use of other words that are related either semantically or phonetically).

Lévi-Strauss's work has been summarized very much in these terms, namely, as a search for unconscious, hidden structuring structures that are analytically comparable to a grammar in that they generate variable (religious and cultural) forms that are in turn analytically comparable to speech. And, in his famous essay on the myth of Oedipus (1993b), the influence of Saussure is immediately apparent: the myth is not to be read simply as a narrative that unfolds diachronically. Instead, the narrative is suspended and key events ('bundles of events' or, elsewhere, 'mythemes') are extracted as the proper subject matter of the analysis:

> It is impossible to understand a myth as a continuous sequence. This is why we should be aware that if we try to read a myth as we read a novel or a newspaper article, that is line after line, reading from left to right, we don't understand the myth, because we have to apprehend it as a totality and discover that the basic meaning of the myth is not conveyed by the sequence of events but – if I may say so – by bundles of events although these events appear at different moments in the story. Therefore, we have to read the myth more or less as we would read an orchestral score, not stave after stave, but understanding that we should apprehend the whole page and understand that something which was written on the first stave at the top of the page acquires meaning only if one considers that it is part and parcel of what is written below on the second stave, the third stave, and so on. That is, we have to read not only from left to right, but at the same time

vertically, from top to bottom. We have to understand that each page is a totality. And it is only by treating the myth as if it were an orchestral score, written stave after stave, that we can understand it as a totality, that we can extract the meaning out of the myth. (Lévi-Strauss 2001: 40)

Lévi-Strauss's method of reading horizontally and vertically draws upon Saussure's model of language with its syntagmatic and paradigmatic dimensions, but also Vladimir Propp's formalism and his earlier work on fairy tales (see Hawkes 1983: 67). However, it also points to Lévi-Strauss's fascination with music (Tremlett 2008a: 58–61) and a more general but important eclecticism: structuralism, as will be seen momentarily, cannot be reduced to its linguistic or Saussurean inheritances.

Once extracted, the 'bundles of events' or 'mythemes' are re-composed into binary oppositions that are then compared to other versions of the same myth or other myths from the same cultural area, because

to study a myth is to study the relationships of 'transformation' ... between the different versions of the myth and between the myth and other myths. With this approach, neither a single version nor a synthesis of several versions is an appropriate object of study. A myth should be considered, rather, as the set of all its versions. (Sperber 1996: 27)

In *The Raw and the Cooked* (1992), Lévi-Strauss states that he will treat 'the sequences of each myth, and the myths themselves in respect of their reciprocal interrelations, like the instrumental parts of a musical work', studying them 'as one studies a symphony' (1992: 26). The book begins with an 'Overture' and continues through a series of variations, symphonies, solos, fugues and a chorus. Lévi-Strauss claims classical music emerged with the decline of myth in Western societies and, with an almost Nietzschean flourish – if we remember that for the early Nietzsche, Wagner's work stood out against the disintegrative, centrifugal forces of modernity – adds that both myth and music 'are instruments for the obliteration of time' (1992: 16).

In *The Raw and the Cooked*, Lévi-Strauss argues that a number of apparently distinct Amerindian myths drawn from a wide geographical and cultural area about the origins of fire, the origins of wild pigs and the origins of tobacco are actually interrelated, and indeed are variations or kaleidoscopic transformations of one another. The upshot of these allusions and pronouncements is an approach to myth that breaks entirely from previous assumptions about the function of myth in early societies and their meaning. If Carl Jung and Joseph Campbell had claimed that the study of myth revealed universal, psychological archetypes which pointed to deep and profound ontological meanings about human existence and possibilities for well-being, Lévi-Strauss re-fashioned the study of myth in terms of a mathematical formula (Lévi-Strauss 1993b: 228) in which the meaning of myth was to be found not in any isolated figure or element but in their combination and transformation. In an interview with the philosopher Didier Eribon, Lévi-Strauss said, 'in everything I have written on mythology I have wanted to show that one never arrives at a final meaning' (Lévi-Strauss and Eribon 1991: 142). According to Lévi-Strauss, myths are authorless and come from nowhere, in the last analysis reflecting not social structure or any spiritual truth, but the (Kantian) mind that generates them. It is for this reason that Lévi-Strauss suggests that his aim is to show 'not how men think in myths, but how myths operate in men's minds without their being aware of the fact', and that his point of departure is not any human 'thinking subject', but instead proceeds 'as if the thinking process were taking place in the myths' (1992: 12).

Importantly, Lévi-Strauss's approach to myths draws not just from linguistics and music, but also from cybernetics and information theory. The myth is a message, and the different versions constitute different transmissions of that message. However, in each transmission, different elements of the message are amplified or distorted or altered in the process. According to Lévi-Strauss, the permutations of myth offer a glimpse into the operations of the mind and its attempts to grapple with a range of philosophical and sociological problems. The myths are messages sent by society to itself in its attempt to resolve the problems it faces – as Lévi-Strauss suggests, 'the purpose of myth is to provide a logical model capable of overcoming a contradiction' – but, precisely because these problems cannot be solved, new versions of the myth continue to be generated 'until the intellectual impulse which … produced it is exhausted' (Lévi-Strauss 1993b: 229). This means that there are no authors, no originals and no copies of these artefacts, only messages without origin, generating variations and transformations that proliferate until they are, finally, exhausted.

Four Christo-Filipino assemblages

I have long been attracted to Marxist and structuralist accounts of change. The insistence – in Marxist accounts – on the centrality of ideology to processes of change, seems undeniable. But the various Marxisms cannot escape their implication in linear, evolutionist and teleological thinking. Wrapped within Marx's stage-like conception of history (that is, a history that proceeds in stages and which is also a kind of theatre in which each character plays a well-defined part) is a chosen subject – the proletariat or working class – that plays a redemptive and eschatological role bringing freedom to all, in almost messianic fashion (this notwithstanding Louis Althusser's attempt to re-construct a Marxism without a subject; see Althusser 2005).

Lévi-Strauss's account of transformation is no less problematic. Whether talking about history or myths, at the centre of Lévi-Strauss's thinking is entropy and the inevitability of dissipation and decay. In *Tristes Tropiques* he declares that the only 'societies we are able to study today' are 'debilitated communities and mutilated social forms' that 'have been shattered by the development of

European civilization, that phenomenon which, for a widespread and innocent section of humanity, has amounted to a monstrous and incomprehensible cataclysm' (2011: 326). But is change inevitably a sad fable of contraction and exhaustion? Might there be found another story at the centre of which is not dissipation or expansion, but creation and transformation?

Before moving on to describe my four Christo-Filipino assemblages, a few words need to be said about how the question of religious and social change in the Philippines has been approached so far in Philippine Studies. Approaches to date have tended to be distinctly modernist in their sensibility albeit implicitly spatial (see Kataoka 2012: 361). For example, an urban–rural distinction has been constitutive of historical and ethnographic works covering both the Spanish and American periods, as a means of distinguishing different experiences of colonization, Christianization and, in the twentieth century, Philippine modernity. As such, accounts of the Christianization of the archipelago have typically distinguished lowland from mountain populations in terms of their differing levels of exposure to evangelization and in terms of the 'little' and the 'great traditions'. These distinctions have enabled contrasts to be drawn between the religiosities of varied peripheries and borderlands at the edge or simply beyond the reach of the colonial town, sometimes taking the perspective of a putative Catholic orthodoxy (Schumacher 2009), sometimes that of a liberal modernity (Sturtevant 1976). The alter-Christianities of the backwoods and the mountains have too often been represented as illegitimate syncretic hybrids of religio-politics and/or as irrational expressions of inchoate political demands.

The question of religion and social change has also been broached with an urban framework, drawing upon studies of Southeast Asia's classical city-states but in relation to conceptions of spiritual and religious power, authority and leadership. The studies in question – notably Robert Heine-Geldern's 'State and Kingship in Southeast Asia' (2006) – assume a significant Indic influence upon the region:

The classical states of Southeast Asia were in theory highly centralized, and embodied ideas, derived from Indian influence, of a divine kingship and of a parallelism between the universe and the terrestrial order. The capital of the ruler was the magical centre of the realm, and at its centre, in turn, a temple or the royal palace, whose towers and terraces and orientation were designed in accordance with an elaborate symbolism, represented Mt. Meru, the abode of the gods. As the kingdom was a microcosm of the universe so the king in his capital, a descendent of a god or an incarnation of a god ... maintained the harmony of the kingdom, matching the harmony of the universe. (Legge 1999: 32)

Benedict Anderson's essay 'The Idea of Power in Javanese Culture' (1972) re-worked some of Heine-Geldern's ideas and applied them to late twentieth-century Indonesian politics, but they were applied elsewhere as well. For example, the Filipino historian R. C. Ileto's careful, textual analysis of nineteenth-century Filipino *pasyon* texts and his discussion of the role of those texts in the 1896 revolution and other uprisings against Spanish and American colonial rule in the nineteenth and early twentieth centuries, draws substantially upon the idea of a pan-Southeast Asian conception of spiritual power. Drawing explicitly on Anderson's work, Ileto's investigations include a meticulous approach to questions of spiritual power (*kapangyarihan*) and interiority (*loób*) in the *pasyon*, with *loób* cast as a space to be cultivated in the process of accumulating *kapangyarihan* (Ileto 2011: 24–5). Herminia Meñez (1999) also draws on Anderson in an essay on post-Marcos Filipino politics, highlighting the role of *anting-anting* (amulets) which, as 'concentrated forms of energy' (1999: 98), are authoritative and highly sought-after symbols and repositories of power for political leaders (cf. Sidel 1999). For both Ileto and Meñez, religious ideas about power and prowess – ideas long divorced from their articulation with the classical city states of the early history of the region –

constitute a kind of cultural constant for explaining certain features of Filipino and wider Southeast Asian politics.[1]

More explicitly spatial and geographical approaches to the Philippines, though they may explore questions of change, tend not to be interested much in religions. Morley's (2018) study of American urbanism in the archipelago supplements a small number of articles and books (for example, see Connell 1999; Shatkin 2005; Ortega 2016) seeking to document the urban history of the country. An exception is Jose Mario C. Francisco's article 'Mapping Religious and Civil Spaces in Traditional and Charismatic Christianities in the Philippines' (2010). Francisco is interested in what he calls the 'construction of sacred space by particular religious institutions' and how these constructions constitute expressions of each group's 'self-understanding' (2010: 215), shaping their engagements with other religious groups and the wider sphere of civil society (2010: 187). In what follows, I interrogate three of the four spaces selected by Francisco for analysis, except that I treat them as assemblages and sever the link made by Francisco between them and self-understanding or subjectivity.

The Philippines 1593 church-plaza assemblage

Urbanization was prevalent in mainland Southeast Asia long before the arrival of Europeans in the region (Keyes 1995). Manila, however, was largely the product of Spanish colonialism, central to which was the process of 'reduction' as prescribed by the Laws of the Indies. These laws, enacted by Philip II in 1573, codified Spanish colonial practices of discovery, settlement and pacification across their colonial possessions, assuring the 'creation of a uniform urban form throughout the entire geographical reach of the Spanish Empire' (Morley 2018: 33). These sixteenth-century ordinances were a combination of Spanish experiences of urbanism in the Americas, classical theories of urbanism, and then contemporary European theories of urban forms, such as that developed by the Renaissance architect and philosopher, Leon Battista Alberti (1404–72) (see Reed 2002: 166; Morley 2018: 34, but also Choay 1997). The ordinances required the re-settlement of the scattered and dispersed indigenous populations of the Philippine archipelago into town centres as a means of concentrating and solidifying Spanish power and facilitating conversion (Francisco 2010: 188). These centres were focused around a church and plaza complex which lay at the heart of a gridded pattern of streets, with the houses of the elite clustered around it. According to Lefebvre,

> These instructions were arranged under the three heads of discovery, settlement and pacification. The very building of the towns thus embodied a plan which would determine the mode of occupation of the territory and define how it was to be reorganized under the political authority of urban power. The orders stipulate exactly how the chosen sites ought to be developed. The result is a strict hierarchical organization of space, a gradual progression outwards from the town centre, beginning with the *ciudad* and reaching out to the surrounding *pueblos*. The plan is followed with geometrical precision: from the inevitable Plaza Mayor a grid extends indefinitely in every direction. Each square or rectangular lot has its function assigned to it, while inversely every function is assigned its own place at a greater or lesser distance from the central square: church, administrative buildings, town gates, squares, streets, port installations, warehouses, town hall, and so on. Thus a high degree of segregation is superimposed upon a homogeneous space ... [It] is also an instrument of production: a superstructure foreign to the original space serves as a political means of introducing a social and economic structure in such a way that it may gain a foothold and indeed establish its 'base' in a particular locality. (Lefebvre 1991: 151; italics in original)

Before the arrival of Spain, Filipinos had lived primarily in dispersed settlements along coasts and rivers, in stark contrast to the already urbanized populations in other regions of Southeast Asia, and these pre-colonial populations were grounded in a unit known as the *barangay*. Re-settlement provided a means to survey Filipino bodies and contain them within Spanish terms of reference:

> The relocation of native bodies – or at least the designation of their areas of residence as parts of a larger administrative grid – permitted them to be identified in Spanish political and religious terms ... The conversion and colonization of the local populace necessitated their physical relocation. Natives had to be taken by either force or persuasion from their dispersed villages and made available to the law's representatives. (Rafael 1988: 90)

In order to facilitate the effective administration and conversion of these peoples, then, it was necessary to up-route these settlements and re-territorialize them in terms of administrative units that made the Church the centre, source and symbol of the colonial regime. From the mid-1580s the development of Manila proceeded apace with the building of a walled city – the Intramuros – which became the religious, political and military seat of Spanish power in the archipelago. By the turn of the seventeenth century it was home to almost 30,000 people (Morley 2018: 36), a symbol of Spanish civilization in stark contrast to the Extramuros where the non-European and indigenous populations lived, in racially zoned quarters. Throughout the seventeenth century the colonial regime organized regular expeditions into frontier parts of Luzon, the Visayas and Mindanao, and these were followed by re-settlement. Like Intramuros, the colonial towns were built on a grid pattern around a church and a central plaza or square. Each new town expanded the network of roads through the territory. The towns themselves functioned like gravitational centres around which clustered the smaller satellite *barrios* and the even smaller, *sitios*. This model of town planning and design functioned as a register of the colonial

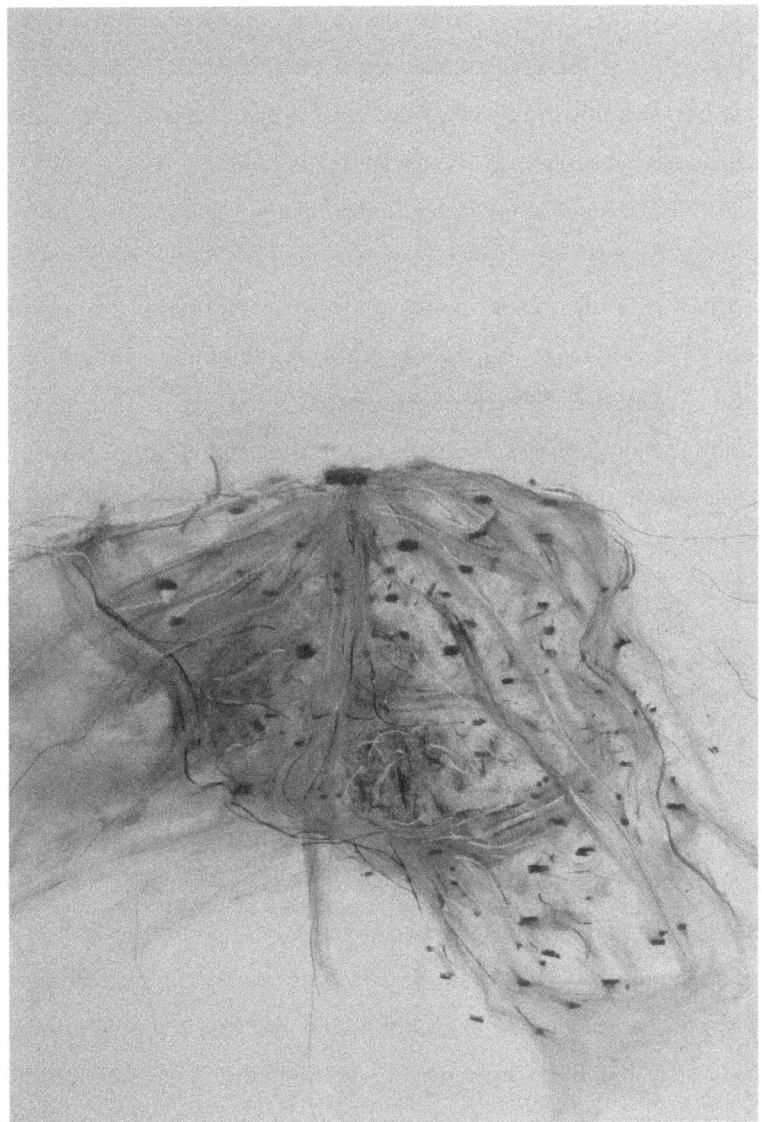

FIGURE 3 *Assemblage 1: The church-plaza assemblage.* © *Atsuhide Ito.*

hierarchy: in each town the church was positioned at the centre, the houses of the local elite around the plaza and the homes of the so-called *indios* at the periphery. Spanish colonial policy depended upon these architectural and planning practices which imposed specific sets of power relations and racial hierarchies between peninsular Spaniards, *mestizos* or those of mixed ancestry, and the *indios*, among which was the injunction that neither Filipino men nor Filipina women could become priests. Emanating from the Church was not simply ecclesiastical power but a particular racialized and gendered morphology of social relationships that did not simply re-route Filipinos out of the pre-colonial *barangay* and into new towns, but also re-rooted them with specific restrictions placed on movement 'so that the natives may not wander about aimlessly when there is no need for it' (Morga 1970: 163). Around the Church were the houses of the *principalía* or local elite, whose children were educated by the priest (Ileto 1998a: 81). According to Ileto, it was 'the priest [who] determined or at least policed the social order in the town' (Ileto 1998a: 82) and presided over its key rituals including baptisms, marriages, funerals and feasts (Ileto 1998a: 80). These occasions were more than ritual moments in an individual biography, or the town or city calendar of feasts and celebrations: they were simultaneously a kind of surveillance.

During the Spanish colonial period, the link between the urban fabric of Filipino towns and cities, and Christianity, was clear. The Laws of the Indies prescribed the construction of the church-plaza complex as the site at which a town or city's most important religious and secular functions would be performed. Ordinance 118 stated that 'here and there in the town, smaller plazas of good proportion shall be laid out, where the temples associated with the principal church, the parish churches and the monasteries can be built, such that everything may be distributed in a good proportion for the instruction of religion' (Mundigo and Crouch 1977: 255). As such, the priest and the Church were not simply symbols of religious power, but the organizing grammar of hierarchies and relations for which the model was a kind of pre-Benthamite panopticon: a spatially orchestrated network of walls and roads, and each of the assemblages detailed in the pages that follow are a translation or variation of it. The Christianization of the Philippines was, then, less a question of conversion – a transmission of discrete beliefs and the instantiation of a religious tradition from one part of the world so that it might become continuous in another – than an articulation of religious practices (baptisms, confession, etc.) with those of town- and city-planning.

But this mode of Christianization generated not a copy of itself as conversion implies, but an entirely new assemblage of objects and things. This assemblage combined and composed Filipino bodies into new proximities and distances, into new relations between and among bodies, with one another and the colonizing power and the rivers, forests and mountains of the archipelago. These combinations and compositions constituted a comprehensive de- and re-territorializing of the islands, generating new insides and outsides and new polarizations, notably between town centres and backwoods peripheries, new frequencies of contact and separation and new kinds of coordinates upon which to plot bodies and information (Deleuze and Guattari 2014: 503). As Arnisson Andre Ortega notes (2016), the programme of re-settlement

> [w]as initiated by Church authorities to purge indigenous residents and forcibly resettle them into … town centres … This forced relocation brought the indigenous population 'under the bells' of Spanish Catholicism and classified them as civilized, lowland Christian *indios*. Politically, this meant the incorporation of the barangay social structure within a colonial administrative hierarchy. Those who refused to submit fled to the mountains and were classified as 'uncivilized' and 'pagan' *remontados*. (Ortega 2016: 130)

The Banahaw assemblage establishes an alternative centre of religious power outside of the town, marked by new flows and new insides and outsides and points to a transition from the solid Religion of the towns and cities to an improvised, liquid religious form at the periphery.

The Philippines 1841 Banahaw assemblage

The authorized religious space of the colonial Philippines was the enclosed grid of the church-plaza assemblage. However, for various reasons – perhaps to escape taxes, the constabulary or the friars – various kinds of 'third space' (Lahiri 2005: 36) emerged at the periphery of the new towns and cities of the archipelago:

> Spanish colonial rule had delineated cities, towns (pueblos) and provincial boundaries within an administrative structure that looked good on paper. In actuality, a mandala-like situation existed wherein the prestige and power of the parish priest and indigenous town élite (*principalia*) determined a pueblo-centre's hold over the peripheries. Up to fairly late in the century, there was ample scope for non-pueblo elements – called hermits, bandits, wanderers, curers, heretics and the like – to operate almost at will, attracting people to them during periods of natural calamities or annual pilgrimages, or forming permanent communities beyond the pueblos. (Ileto 1999: 207; italics in original)

Mount Banahaw was one such space, and it emerged out of the bloody aftermath of a religious uprising.

The Cofradia de San José was founded by Apolinario de la Cruz who worked as an orderly in the San Juan hospital in Manila. Having been prevented from joining the priesthood on racial grounds, he established his own religious fraternity. Intended only for Filipinos, the Cofradia was founded in 1832 but only became a rebellion once efforts to achieve official recognition were exhausted. In October 1840 the Cofradia petitioned the Archbishop of Manila, requesting ecclesiastical recognition. When this was rejected, a second petition was sent to the Royal Audiencia but this too was rejected, effectively criminalizing the Cofradia, its activities and membership. De la Cruz led his followers to the slopes of Mount San Cristobel, one of a pair of extinct volcanoes, and established a camp. His followers declared him

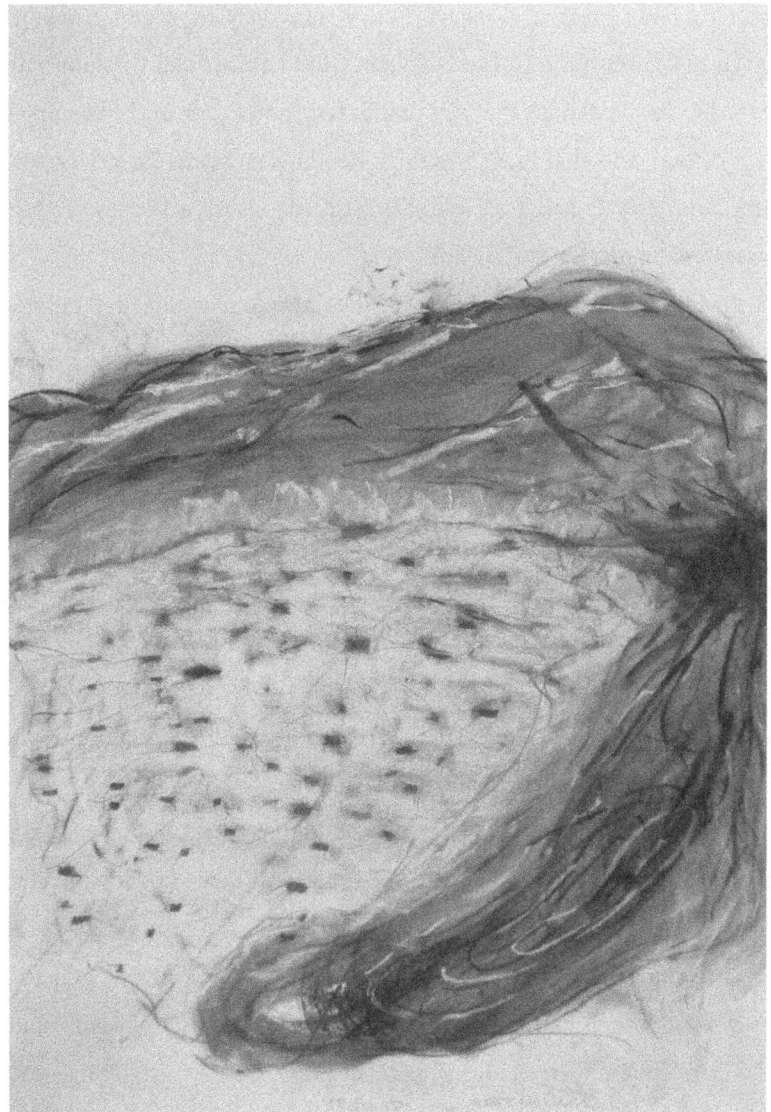

FIGURE 4 *Assemblage 2: The Banahaw assemblage.* © *Atsuhide Ito.*

'King of the Tagalogs' (Ileto 2011: 58), but his reign was brief. In 1841 the rebellion was crushed as government troops overran the camp. Apolinario de la Cruz escaped to the dense forests of San Cristobel's sister peak Mount Banahaw, but he was captured soon after and, along with 200 of his followers, executed (see Sweet 1970). In 1870, Spanish government reports noted that

Apolinario had appeared, along with the Virgin Mary, to several people urging them to re-establish the Cofradia. When I did fieldwork in the mountains in 1999–2000, locals told me that Apolinario returned as one of the *Santong Boces* (Holy Voices), and that these voices guided later pilgrims including Amador Suarez, who established the Ciudad Mistica de Dios on the lower slopes of Mount Banahaw in the early 1950s.

A key feature of the Cofradia, and the various religious and millenarian insurrections of the nineteenth-century Philippines, was how conceptions of spiritual power and notions of millenarian, apocalyptic time combined to up-route 'families ... from the often closely knit kinship systems of the towns', separating 'men and women ... from their spouses, children or parents', to bring them 'together in a new society' (Ileto 2011: 60). According to Ileto, these uprisings and the communities they established provided the possibility of 'not just a counterculture, but a counterstructure' (Ileto 1999: 194) to the Spanish colonial state. These counter-structures emerged around a charismatic leader whose claims authorized the irruption of these other, millenarian temporalities and animistic conceptions of power.

In 'Rural Life in a Time of Revolution' (1998a) Ileto juxtaposes some of the Spanish towns of the provinces of Laguna and Quezon (Tiaong, Dolores, Sariaya and San Pablo City) with Mount Banahaw and Mount San Cristobel, describing the latter as 'a third realm' (Ileto 1998a: 85). According to Ileto, both the towns with their churches and priests at their centres – like the mountain in their midst with their *manggagamot* (healers), *supremas* (religious leaders), *mangkukulam* (sorcerers) and their reputation as a repository for powerful objects known as *anting-anting* (amulets) – constitute competing gravitational centres dependent upon different forms of energy to draw and maintain people and things in their orbit. Importantly, Ileto does not simply oppose these different attractors – the lowland town as against the upland counter-structure – but highlights the extent to which Filipinos flowed across these different spaces:

When ... our gaze shifts from Manila ... to the rural areas affected by the revolution, we encounter experiences and narratives that the linear history of our nation-state would find hard put to accommodate. Instead of a straightforward transition from colonial darkness to the light of independence, we find peoples of the Philippines shifting their identities under changing circumstance, juggling their loyalties among state, family, and church, and mixing up the modern categories of 'religious' and 'secular'. (Ileto 1998a: 97–8)

Today, the mountain is widely known for the 'Rizalist' churches on its lower slopes, so-called for their veneration of the national hero José Rizal, as the Filipino Christ. Rizal, a well-travelled and well-educated Filipino novelist and doctor, was executed in Manila in 1896 but later elevated by the Americans to the status of national hero, and monuments were built in his memory across the archipelago. In a survey of various Rizalist groups, movements and churches, Foronda (1961) argues that their beliefs and practices are evidence for the persistence, among 'the poor unlettered folk ... living in mountain areas and far-flung barrios' (1961: 37) of an indigenous, pre-Hispanic ancestor worship. This argument denies the novelty of Rizalism as a new religious formation, with its own material culture and its reversal of the gendered and racialized morphology of the church-plaza assemblage.

One Rizalist church – the Ciudad Mistica de Dios or Mystical City of God – moved to Banahaw in the 1950s, its leader Amador Suarez having reportedly been guided by the *Santong Boces*. The community has since constructed a large compound that includes two churches, an infirmary, a workshop, a residence for their leader with rooms for guests as well as quarters for around forty nuns and a large kitchen and refectory. These are located at the centre of the compound and, around the edge, living quarters for followers have been built. The key components of the Law of Indies are present: the power lies at the compound's centre, radiating outwards like the rays of the sun. Additionally, the roof of the main building is in the shape of a dove with outstretched wings, symbolizing the presence of the Holy Spirit. Mistica's construction of a 'city' in Mount Banahaw is precisely an attempt to establish a counter-urbanism – a new Jerusalem, if you will – on a mountain they claim has eschatological significance with a basis in scripture. However, Mistica's significance goes further: as well as challenging the racial hierarchies of religious authority and constituting a novel form of religious urbanization,[2] Mistica is also notable for its female *Suprema* and the location of spiritual legitimacy in her and a cadre of nuns (Quibuyen 1991).

According to Ileto (1998b), the veneration and remembering of Rizal by groups such as Ciudad Mistica de Dios and the Spiritual Filipino Catholic Church subvert state and official commemorations of the national hero. For Lahiri (2002), however, the veneration and remembering of Rizal by religious groups and movements signifies the colonization of former border areas like Mount Banahaw and their transformation into ideological props for official nationalism (see Tremlett 2008b). However, I would suggest that the monuments to Rizal built on the slopes of Mount Banahaw point to a more complex state of affairs that includes the appropriation of a secular aesthetic of urban design brought to the Philippines by Daniel Burnham and his assistant, Peirce Anderson, as they set about introducing a new kind of urbanism to the Philippines.

At the heart of Spanish rule had been the Intramuros with its morphology of walls and sharp divides between the inside and the outside – a taxonomy and a mode of administration, set in solid stone. The City Beautiful aesthetic brought to the Philippines by Burnham transformed the look and feel of the capital. First, the centre of Manila was shifted to the Extramuros. Second, new roads and boulevards, green spaces, public buildings and monuments were built, with the intention to facilitate 'people to freely see public offices, observe civic rituals and intermingle' (Morley 2018: 79) in ways that had not been possible during the Spanish period. Third, the construction of a Rizal monument as a focal point for national pride and the invention of a civic ritual

FIGURE 5 *Rizal monument outside the Spiritual Filipino Catholic Church on Mount Banahaw: note the angle of the head. Source: author.*

calendar to mark Rizal's life and death became key elements of a wider strategy of urban design to promote 'moral, intellectual and governmental progress' (Morley 2018: 49). With regard to the latter, Rizal monuments were also constructed in towns up and down the country, becoming civic ritual sites in their own right.

Importantly, the monuments to Rizal built on the slopes of Mount Banahaw depict him in almost the same terms as the official monuments, that is, in the same Western attire and heroic, rigid pose and elevated upon impressive concrete plinths. As such, these representations reproduce quintessentially modern elements of early twentieth-century American monumental architecture on the mountain. Additionally, the angle of Rizal's head suggests a nod – excuse the pun – to baroque depictions of another Filipino hero and the suturing together of multiple elements poached from multiple sources.

Certainly for the Americans, the monumental representation of Rizal's body as an object of discipline and restraint was a means of reproducing and transmitting the Protestant masculinity of the period with its emphasis on virtues such as courage, discipline, independence, strength and will, among others. According to Nagel (1998), this masculinity in concrete is linked in

FIGURE 6 *Rizal monument in the garden of the church plaza in San Pablo City: note the angle of the head. Source: author.*

complex ways with the emergence of nationalism, capitalism and processes of modernization. In the Banahaw assemblage, these elements are reconfigured and re-situated among a range of new and improvised features, pointing to the mountain as a site of religious improvisation and experimentation.

The Philippines 1967 arcadian assemblage

The other of both the church-plaza assemblage with its closed, urban forms, and (to anticipate somewhat) the media-church assemblage with its distributed and open, rhizomatic connectivities, is the arcadian assemblage. This assemblage also represents a development of the Banahaw assemblage: whereas the Banahaw assemblage reversed the racialized and gendered morphology of the church-plaza assemblage, the arcadian assemblage generates its form from pure resistance to urban modernity, framed partly in terms of a Vatican II theology of romantic re-enchantment but also from local discourses of simplicity and authenticity and a new eco-theology (Bulloch 2017; Gariguez 2008).

In the Philippines a political theology emerged, initially, as a response to the economic and political crises of the countryside in the 1950s, developing into a leftist theology in the 1970s and, more recently, into a fully-fledged eco-theology oriented towards Catholic revitalization, routed through a celebration of Filipino indigenous forms of life and knowledge. Giordano (1988) has detailed the post-Vatican II period within the Church in the Philippines, identifying a resolve among certain elements within the Church to tackle widespread problems of poverty, economic and political inequality, and abuses of human rights committed by the army and police. According to Giordano, the creation of the National Secretariat of Social Action (NASSA) under the direction of Bishop Labayen in 1967 led to the adoption of increasingly critical positions by elements within the Church towards the government.

This period also saw the founding of the group Christians for National Liberation, which shared the Philippine Communist Party's (CPP) analysis

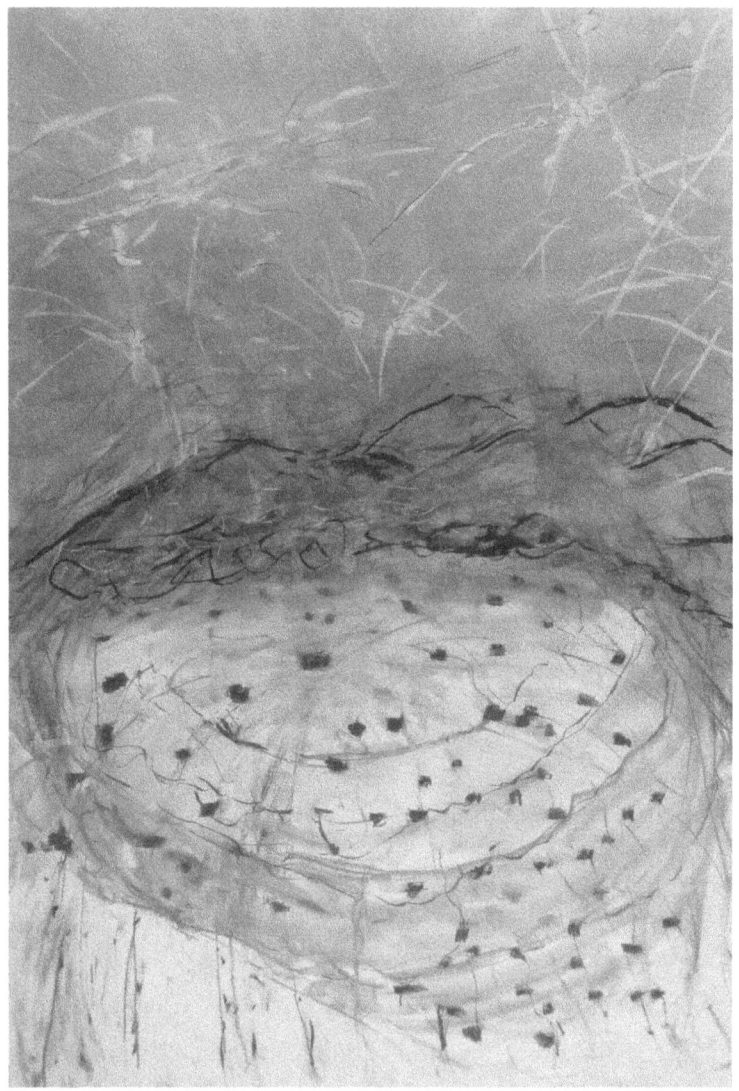

FIGURE 7 *Assemblage 3: The arcadian assemblage.* © Atsuhide Ito.

of society regarding both its structural problems and some of the solutions to those problems. Indeed, after Ferdinand E. Marcos's declaration of martial law in 1972 an increasing number of priests, seminarians and religious began actively co-operating with the National Democratic Front (NDF), while others even took up arms within the ranks of the New People's Army (NPA).

In the 1930s, Filipino communists had branded priests and seminarians 'clericofascists' (Bolasco 1994a: 235), believing that the Church was a feudal remnant destined to wither away and die once the revolution had taken place. Indeed, the Catholic Church's support for Franco during the Spanish civil war (1936–39) saw the Church, during this period, firmly and actively aligned against communism, understood as a dangerously virulent kind of secularism. Likewise, during the 1950s, the dominant position within the Church was to resist all tendencies towards the secularization of Philippine society. Secularization, it was thought, would fatally weaken the country's moral fabric and precipitate a communist take-over. However, Marcos's declaration of martial law in 1972 led some elements within the Church in the Philippines – elements already radicalized by Vatican II – to enter into dialogue with other religious groupings and with the NDF:

Priests, nuns, seminarians, pastors and young Christian men and women were already distancing themselves from accepted Church patterns of social action. In their search for alternatives, this ecumenical grouping finally met face to face the Marxists they had been trained to fear for decades. Less defensively, they faced the concrete challenge of Maoism to the Filipino Christian. Through 1971 they probed. On September 1971, during a seminar in Baguio hosted by Protestants, the organisation-movement Christians for National Liberation (CNL) was formalised ... In February 1972, following a two-day seminar, the CNL formally declared its alignment with the National Democratic Front (NDF). In August 1972, they had their first national assembly. In 1974, CNL was declared a mass organisation tasked with waging a 'national democratic and cultural revolution particularly in the areas of liturgy, theology and religious life'. It was a struggle for the 'social appropriation of the gospel'. (Bolasco 1994a: 247)

The Church would later play a pivotal role in the uprising that led to ignominious exile for Marcos and his family (see also Bolasco 1994b; Guan

2018: 190). However, once 'People Power' had been asserted, the Church hierarchy formally distanced itself from the NDF and the CNL. Nevertheless, the legacy of Church engagement with the poor had engendered a series of theological experiments in which engagement with the rural and the local had occupied centre stage. Heather Lynn Claussen (2001), for example, provides a detailed account of the Missionary Benedictine Sisters, nuns radicalized by Vatican II and the climate of the Marcos period. Claussen highlights their regular trips to Mount Banahaw to visit the *Suprema* and the Ciudad Mistica de Dios. Claussen's 'unconventional' sisters are, among other things, engaged in a quest for a Filipina feminism routed through accounts of the pre-Hispanic Philippines with its mythologized female religious specialists and leaders, as well as through the example of contemporary female religious leaders such as Mistica's own *Suprema*.

Jesuit theologians have also been making the trip to Mount Banahaw as a means of re-thinking their own approaches to the improvised and extra-institutional religiosities and spiritualities that exist in spaces such as Mount Banahaw:

The study [of local Filipino religiosities] arose out of a seminar-workshop at the Loyola School of Theology, Ateneo de Manila University, during the first semester of 1979. The participants were trying to apply Lonergan's 'Method in Theology' to specific problems of inculturation in the Philippines. The problems were tentatively contextualised as a polarisation between two cultures – the more Westernised and the less Westernised Filipino cultures, between the urbanised minority and the rural majority of the Christian population, between official religion and popular religiosity. This cultural polarisation was seen as a significant aspect of the country's four centuries of colonial history. The participants agreed that studies of popular piety before Vatican II, although well-documented, lacked the insights into the cultural pluralism of Vatican II; these uncritically assumed that the culture of medieval Western Europe or the modern technocratic culture of industrialised nations was the 'norm' for all other cultures, and that cultural progress consisted in making these other cultures conform to the 'norm'. Historically, as a result of this assumption, some expressions of the people's search for God and the faith are despised and pejoratively labelled as 'popular religiosity' or 'folk Christianity'. Pope Paul VI has since exhorted Catholics, in *Evangelii Nuntiandi*, to rediscover the positive elements in popular piety and to purify it of its negative elements. (Marasigan 1985: 1)

Vicente Marasigan sets out an opposition that he claims was characteristic of documents on so-called 'popular piety' prepared before Vatican II. These documents distinguished between urban and rural populations and between an urban minority in the Philippines cast as the bearer of 'official religion' and a rural majority which had remained, somehow, inadequately 'inculturated'. In other words, a position was advanced in those documents whereby the rural Philippines continued to be a missionary space, a space that, for a whole host of complex reasons, had remained beyond the pastoral project of the Church. In this analysis, 'folk Christianity' was, as it were, a poor copy or imitation of an official master religion that required urgent theological correction.

Marasigan's critique of these arguments stresses the need for 'participant observation' and 'immersion experiences' (1985: 2) of the kind he himself experienced, living and conducting research in Mount Banahaw, and his claim that the people who reside there live 'very close to nature and ... [are] extremely sensitive to its beauties and changing moods, and they commune with nature in a very intimate way, almost intersubjectively' (1985: 3).

Filipino students and academics now travel regularly to the mountain as part of various study programmes. Vitaliano Gorospe's coffee-table style book *Banahaw: Conversations with a Pilgrim to the Power Mountain* (1992) includes maps and photographs of the various shrines and the pilgrimage routes around the lower slopes of the mountain, while his discussion of the religious lives of those who live on Banahaw is framed explicitly in terms of an opposition of rural life versus city or urban living. It is assumed that those who live close to nature have unmediated access to the divine and authentic spiritual experience in a way that is simply not open to city dwellers:

> Nature reminds us that we need to have moments of stillness and harmony with our whole self so that we can come closer to nature and its Creator and thus discover our own true selves. Some think that going to Banahaw is an escape from reality found in the city. On the contrary, it is the city that is artificial and Banahaw that is natural. We were not meant to live like a thousand chickens cooped in cement cages and choked by smog and deafened by urban noise. When we first encounter Banahaw we will find the stillness it demands very strange; we are not ready to surrender to nature and its Creator. (Gorospe 1992: 73)

Importantly, Gorospe is not grappling, as was Marasigan before him, with the legacy of pre-Vatican II theology. Today Banahaw is a site less for theological error than for a deeper theological truth in which 'prayer before a rock, prayer while bathing in the stream, prayer inside the cave, [and] prayer among the trees and the stars' pose the possibility of 'a higher and deeper journey – a journey to our spirituality' (Gorospe 1992: 70).

If there are any doubts as to the purchase of theological and indeed elite intellectual discourses with currents of popular Filipino culture, these ideas in fact mesh very closely with contemporary ideas about rural simplicity and authenticity and what Hannah Bulloch calls the idea of the 'simple life' (Bulloch 2017: 15), which she documents from fieldwork she conducted in Siquijor. The 'simple life' is, according to Bulloch, a local discourse that favours 'austerity over consumer culture and attention to social relationships over attention to making money' (2017: 49) and it has considerable appeal across a range of socio-economic strata. This discourse emerged through fieldwork conversations about development, progress, work and mobility, constituting a moral economy if you will through which, according to Bulloch, Filipinos evaluate themselves in relation to others both near and far.

Bulloch describes the discourse of the simple life as a 'bucolic ideal' (ibid.) and it can be seen as tinged with nostalgia for an uncomplicated rural way of life. In fact the Philippines was profoundly transformed as a landscape through colonial and post-colonial projects such as urbanism, intensive agriculture, tourism and mining. Contemporary eco-theologians approach these processes as a kind of 'unmapping' wherein landscapes once alive and animated by meaningful relations between peoples, animals, places and secret spots were reconfigured as empty (Tsing 2005: 28–9). Church groups and NGOs, in response to developments from resource extraction to housing, are increasingly combining a post-Vatican II theology of political engagement with a new eco-theology. Fundamental to this new approach is the anxiety that nature – both in a quantitative sense that articulates concern for entities such as trees, rivers, mountains, oceans, birds, fish, monkeys and so forth, but also in a qualitative sense that encompasses relationships not just between people but also between people and trees, animals, rivers, mountains and oceans – is being replaced as a co-ordinating dwelling place by an artifice of concrete, steel and glass. The textures and relational connectivities that these artificial surfaces enable are understood to be quite un-natural and de-humanizing. As the Filipino theologian Edwin Gariguez observes, 'the ecological problem [in the Philippines] is but part of the present alienation of the human person', an alienation that stems from a (Western) 'mechanistic and materialistic point of view' that reduces all decisions to a 'market utilitarian calculus' (Gariguez 2008: 4). Environmental degradation will follow – as surely as night follows day – when and where 'the prosperity and security of the greater global economy takes priority over local needs and the personal anxiety of achievement overtakes the integrity of community' (Walpole 2010: iv). Thus there emerges a powerful sense that if economic development is not fundamentally re-oriented, certain natural connectivities and relationships will become lost or extinct. But what are these other connectivities? And where are they to be found? And why should anyone care about the possibility or indeed likelihood of their demise?

Short answers to the above questions are quite straightforward. First, the other connectivities in question refer to a religious sensibility that accords the environment, and its species, trees, rivers, mountains and oceans, a sacred significance. Second, this sensibility is said to be found structuring the life-ways of indigenous groups living in the so-called 'ancestral domains'. Third, the extinction of these life-ways would be calamitous because it would represent a further diminution of cultural and natural variety but, perhaps more importantly, it would also constitute the disappearance of a form or way of life that, for Filipino theologians like Gariguez, has the potential to renew and revitalize human relationships not simply with the natural environment but with God.

A distinctive feature, then, of the arcadian assemblage is the entanglement of tropes of 'alienation' and 'authenticity' not just in relation to the city but also in relation to the archipelago's indigenous peoples. For eco-theologians such as Gariguez, the indigenous peoples have become signifiers of re-enchantment as well as of ecological sustainability. According to Gariguez,

> Ecological spirituality is not a newly-discovered path or perspective. On the contrary, this kind of spirituality that respects the intimate relationship with the earth had been part of the traditions of the indigenous peoples since time immemorial and had been a constitutive motif of their culture, beliefs and their very identity as a people. (2008: 29)

In fact, indigenous connectivity with nature – with other species, other humans and the land – is configured in terms of two idioms: first, *buhay ay*

FIGURE 8 *Urban street vendor in Malate, Manila selling paintings depicting a bucolic ideal of the Filipino countryside. Source: author.*

lupa at lupa ay buhay and second, *inang kalikasan*. The first means 'life is earth and earth is life' while the second means, simply, 'mother nature'.

Buhay ay lupa at lupa ay buhay posits an essential connectivity between human life and well-being and the natural environment, in which the well-being of humans and the environment is constituted reciprocally and relationally. It constitutes nature as the source of authentic sustenance for all peoples. The earth is a form of sustenance that urban dwellers have been detached from, but which remains real for indigenous peoples. The well-being of the earth in like fashion depends on what is framed as an ethic of 'stewardship' that is said to be practised by indigenous peoples. This ethic of stewardship arises from the idea that the landscape and its trees, rivers, mountains and oceans are inherently sacred. Indeed, according to Gariguez, 'the ancestral domain comprises of interacting landscapes of human community, nature ecosystems and the living spirits of the land, which include also the spirits of their ancestors' (Gariguez 2008: 212). The presence of the ancestors in the landscape suggests a temporal dimension to this ethic which stretches backwards in time in a way that renders the living responsible for maintaining the dwelling places of the ancestors which include the same forests, rivers, mountains and oceans that are targets for various forms of resource extraction. This tradition of stewardship is also projected forwards in time to include the unborn as future inhabitants and custodians of the ancestral dwelling places.

Inang kalikasan suggests that the relationship between nature and human beings is an analogue of the relationship enjoyed between a mother and her children. For Filipinos, that relationship is or ought to be defined by respect by juniors for seniors, and for a duty of care between them that creates a cycle of reciprocity between the mother and her offspring. This 'folk' theory of ethical stewardship is glossed by Church activists in such a way that it appears to intersect with Catholic theological conceptions of the allegedly proper mode for human relationships with God and to God's creation. Accordingly, 'the salvation of our civilization and Christian religious tradition may well depend on our ability to draw insights from the tribal religious experience which will help us recover the presence of God in creation and live lightly on the earth' (Gariguez 2008: 8).

Perhaps the arcadian assemblage is more an imaginary made up of odds and ends of discourse and culture, rather than any real place. But even if this is conceded, it nevertheless points to empirical processes of decomposition at work particularly upon the church-plaza assemblage, and constitutes a definite acceleration of the Banahaw assemblage.

The Philippines 2009 media-church assemblage

The regime of Ferdinand Marcos (1917–89) is probably most famous outside the Philippines for tales of corruption, murder and shoes, as well as the so-called People Power Revolution to which the regime eventually succumbed (see Hamilton-Paterson 1999). Less well-known is Marcos's proclamation of the 'New Society' and his ambitious plans to modernize the country. A number of flagship urban projects were launched in Manila including clearances of informal settlements and the construction of the Cultural Centre Complex (CCC), which today houses the Cultural Centre of the Philippines and which was built on reclaimed land on Manila Bay (Connell 1999: 420). Marcos's development of Manila intensified a process that had begun with Daniel Burnham, namely, the decalcification of the church-plaza assemblage.

According to Neferti Tadiar (1995), during the Marcos years Manila was a low-rise city that, unlike Paris, London or New York, denied residents 'an aerial perspective' (Tadiar 1995: 285). But after 'the toppling of the Marcos dictatorship and the much-touted restoration of democracy ... a new metropolitan form that is altering the face of the metropolis and the experience of its spaces ... emerged: "flyovers"' (1995: 286). According to Tadiar, the meaning of flyovers exceeds technocratic attempts to de-congest Manila's traffic. Precisely because the flyovers make possible new perspectives on the city, new experiences and psychological states become possible (1995: 287).

Tadiar's suggestive claim that roads and flyovers might be implicated in urban and psychological transformation is important because, after the fall of Marcos and in particular from the late 1990s, Manila has seen an explosion in urban development, including shopping malls, gated communities, high-rise condominiums and luxury hotels. The urban coordinates, frequencies and polarizations generated by these new spatial forms constitute an immense transformation of the church-plaza assemblage and, embedded in this new, distributed urban morphology, is El Shaddai (see Ortega 2016: 167–88).

El Shaddai is a new, Filipino religious form that combines charismatic Pentecostalism, 'with its emphasis on the power and the visible and audible gifts of the Holy Spirit' (Walls 2010: 146), with local Filipino practices, particularly indigenous conceptions of power and healing (Wiegele 2006: 499).

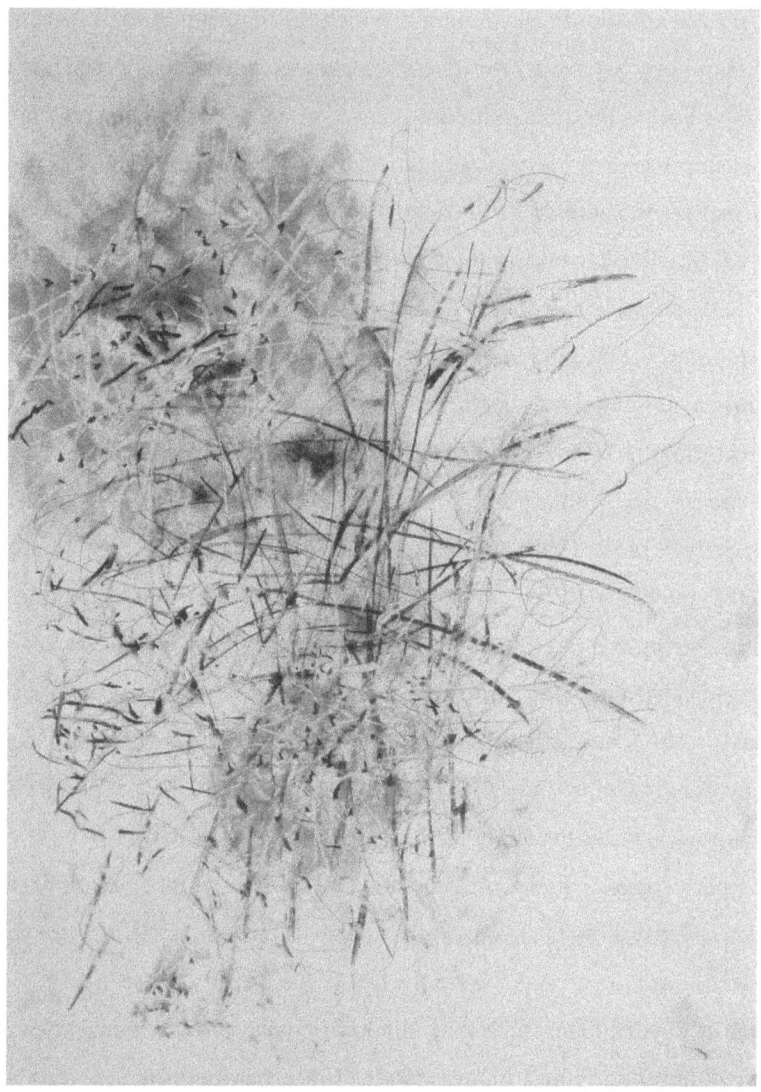

FIGURE 9 *Assemblage 4: The media-church assemblage.* © *Atsuhide Ito.*

Entrepreneurial, enthusiastic, visceral (Meyer 2010) and with the stress firmly placed on the immediacy and presence of the Holy Spirit, El Shaddai travels not merely by road but by radio, television and social media to reach new people in new ways. Its modes of transmission bypass those of the church-plaza assemblage as the traditional space of religious reproduction.

El Shaddai's popularity points to the transformation of the church-plaza assemblage, away from the emphasis on hierarchically enclosed spaces to a new emphasis on media, mobility and flatter space (many Filipinos live and work outside the country, and constitute a huge diasporic audience for El Shaddai). Francisco (2010) notes that El Shaddai 'grew out of a radio program[me] hosted by Mariano "Mike" Velarde and now counts nine to eleven million followers in the Philippines and abroad ... This extensive reach is made possible by its construction of virtual religious space through a unique interplay of mass media and community' (Francisco 2010: 201). Wiegele argues in similar fashion:

> From its inception the community has been, to a large extent, a mass-mediated community. Even though El Shaddai outdoor rallies and other events are now also experienced live, mass media actually produce this 'liveness'. It is this predominance of radio and television that differentiates El Shaddai experience from mainstream Catholic experience and helps to create some of its distinctive features – a new form of religious space, new understandings of religious community, and a more personalized relationship with God. (Wiegele 2005: 41)

Key features of El Shaddai practice include prayer meetings (*gawaín*) held in local village chapters, weekly open-air rallies at the grounds of the Philippine International Convention Center (PICC) by Manila Bay, television broadcasts of these rallies, and an almost 24/7 radio presence in Manila and around the country (Wiegele 2006: 497). According to Wiegele (2005: 58), El Shaddai's mass rallies and their transmission on radio and television have extended the 'sacred and ritual space beyond the immediate locale into the ... home'. Although El Shaddai does not require followers to give up their 'traditional attachments' to their parish, nevertheless these 'mass mediated religious practices' point to spatial transformations in

Filipino towns and cities up and down the archipelago. El Shaddai is a new kind of Filipino Christianity that actively develops 'global networks' that are not 'tied to one privileged locality' (Meyer 2010: 742). It is, as such, the other of the church-plaza assemblage, formed not from a colonial, pan-optic urban morphology of insides and outsides but rather from the transversal, rhizomatic connectivities of the global city (Sassen 2005). In 2009, El Shaddai opened a mega-church in Parañaque City, near Manila. This 'International House of Prayer' seats up to 16,000 people and it claims to be the largest centre of worship in Asia (Wiegele 2011: 175). Networked through apps and platforms such as Foursquare and Facebook and architecturally and aesthetically resembling more a mall than the baroque style typical to most Catholic churches in the Philippines, it acts as a node of assembly not to a geographically bounded community but rather to a dispersed, global Filipino population many of whom reside overseas in Hong Kong, Japan, Saudi Arabia, Britain and America. This assemblage form is the polar opposite to the church-plaza assemblage, yet co-exists with it, generating a complex entanglement of lines and spaces. Its overlapping of the closed, walled spaces of the church-plaza assemblage with new virtual, transnational and post-plaza urban spaces points to the acceleration of the decomposition of the church-plaza assemblage.

Assemblages and change

If to study religions is to study flows, it also means studying religions spatially. Flows flow from one space to another, occupying, ebbing and swelling. They cross borders and invoke states. Religions as flows are, as such, deeply political. These flows are not directed or authored by human beings. Rather, they are the complex outcomes of interactions that configure human and non-human elements in continuous processes of interactive transformation. The account

FIGURE 10 *The four assemblages overlaid.* © *Atsuhide Ito.*

of religion and social change developed in this chapter was made in the spirit of Deleuze and Guattari's notion of nomad science (2014: 420–36), that is, as a science of flows, turbulent vortices, active spaces, events and problematics. I sketched four Christo-Filipino assemblages: the first emerged out of the Laws of the Indies, a Spanish colonial policy document which mandated the construction of towns and cities across the new world and the Philippine archipelago and I called it the Philippines 1593 church-plaza assemblage. Filipinos were relocated from their dispersed settlements and concentrated in the new towns and cities as part of a process of Christianization and boundary-making: beyond the evangelized gaze of the town and city inside were the hills, rivers and forests, the yet-to-be-Christianized spaces of the outside. The new towns and cities not only established this inside-outside boundary; they also regulated the gendered and racialized flows and movements across and through it, along the fibrous networks of roads and sea-routes that also plugged the archipelago into an emergent economy of extraction from the colonial periphery to the sovereign centre. The church-plaza assemblage was a founding moment, articulated as if the Philippines was an empty space. The three subsequent assemblages are all variations of it, arising from specific tipping points or phase transitions at which solid states become liquid and mobile.

The second assemblage pulsed in mountain grottos and improvised monuments: I called it the Philippines 1841 Banahaw assemblage. This assemblage was distributed temporally and spatially between historical events beginning with the Cofradia de San José, an uprising which made its final stand around Mount Banahaw in 1841, and in the twentieth century, the serial construction of Rizal monuments in the 1950s. These latter are evidence of the vernacular appropriation of American City Beautiful urbanism and monumentalism, and mark the emergence of an entirely new religion called 'Rizalism'. One of the new, 'Rizalist' churches, the Ciudad Mistica de Dios, also embarked on fabricating its own urban imaginary, a kind of religious urbanization in which a city form was built in a rural location as a site for the establishment of an authentic Christian community for Filipinos, led by a cadre of female religious officers. Together, these events and moments established an alternative to the inside-outside flow regime established by Spain, that would not be substantially altered by the Americans: new circulations and centres of religious knowledge and experience were established that privileged the religious power and authority of Filipino men and women. If a map of this assemblage were to be laid over the top of the church-plaza assemblage it would make visible Mount Banahaw to the missionary gaze of the towns, not as a yet-to-be-Christianized space, but as a counter space of ongoing religious and social improvisation.

A third assemblage, a logical acceleration of its predecessor, emerged in far-flung, rural backwaters inhabited by the marginalized and dispossessed indigenous peoples to become an imaginary of the true Filipino and a site for authentic Christianization: I called it the Philippines 1967 arcadian assemblage. It reversed the inside-outside regime of flows authorized by the church-plaza assemblage, not by borrowing its artefacts and re-circulating them as with the Banahaw assemblage, but by making the outside the inside and the inside the outside. Rural backwater replaced the town as the space of real religion and real community, and vice versa.

The fourth and final assemblage was associated with the rise of another new religion – a Catholic evangelical movement called El Shaddai – and Manila's new urbanism. It spread along radio waves, television programmes, mass rallies, mega-church performances, social media platforms and diasporic communities as well: I called it the Philippines 2009 media-church assemblage. Operating across both physical and virtual spaces, it added a new layer of global, networked complexity to the inside-outside regime of flows initially put in place by the church-plaza assemblage.

Each assemblage formed a pattern with the church-plaza assemblage constituting the root pattern and, when these patterns are overlaid, one on top of the other, a kaleidoscopic effect is generated to reveal re-alignments of old elements and the generation of new ones. Importantly, the changes appear to be the property of the assemblages themselves. It is to be remembered that the assemblages do not form a temporal sequence whereby one assemblage replaces the previous one: rather, they all exist at the same time. Looking at religion and social change in this way does not enable the discernment of the direction of change – it is not a theory with a predictive or a teleological dimension – however, it does enable a new account of change which is premised on pinpointing the transitions between each state which does not need the subject or indeed any kind of essence or substance to hold it together.

4

Emergence

Introduction

In the previous chapter I was concerned with generative interactivity as a spatially and indeed urban, transformative process. In this chapter my focus on generative interaction continues. Here I describe a Cargo Cult assemblage at the centre of which lies a cosmic geography encompassing the lands of the living and the lands of the dead. In order to understand how the Cargo Cult assemblage formed, I use the notion of emergence which refers to moments when 'interactions disrupt, causing the system to differentiate and ultimately coalesce into something novel' (Holman 2010: 18). Emergence is more than just a term denoting the appearance of a new thing or phenomenon. Indeed, the appearance of a thing or phenomenon is not emergence if that thing or phenomenon could be predicted in advance from the interactions of its elements. Rather, the appearance of a thing or phenomenon is only emergence if something new emerges (Corning 2012).

I begin the chapter with an exploration of two theories of religious experience and creativity that have been used to think about religious change and innovation. They fall under the purview of the lived religion thesis, but here their explanatory power will be assessed in relation to the 'Vailala Madness' (Williams 1977) and the emergence of so-called Cargo Cults in

Melanesia in the early decades of the twentieth century. The first theory refers to Max Weber's conception of charisma, an effervescent explosion of energy and power that is so disruptive of quotidian experience that it shatters traditional and rational forms of authority and legitimacy to usher in something extraordinary and unequivocally new. The second has been drawn piece-meal from sources such as Lévi-Strauss's notion of *bricolage* and the Russian literary theorist Mikhail Bakhtin and his notion of dialogism. Both have been used to explore everyday acts of borrowing, blending and improvising such as those described by Robert Orsi in *The Madonna of 115th Street*, who argued that lived religion is a kind of 'cultural work' (2002: xix) that engages the body and the imagination in a kind of 'religious creativity' (2002: xxiii). Importantly, lying at the centre of both is precisely what this book has set out to get beyond: the meaning-endowing or rational-choice making subject. As an alternative, the concept of emergence will envision the emergence of the Cargo Cults assemblage – the appearance of which, at the time, could only be explained in terms of tropes of madness and contagion – by mapping the entanglements of a series of historically contingent elements including colonialism, plantations and capitalist extraction, indigenous religion and culture, Protestant mission and racism but also the Bible, copra, radios and the dead.

Religious experience and creativity

In volume one of *Economy and Society* (1978) Max Weber constructed four ideal types of social action peculiar to those societies that had undergone the transition to modernity. In particular Weber argued that it was rational action or instrumental rationality that had come to increasingly pervade the cultures and societies of the West in the political-bureaucratic and economic spheres, but also surging beyond these areas and into everyday life. In *The Protestant Ethic and the Spirit of Capitalism* (2002), Weber sought to understand the origins of this rational-instrumental form of social action, and postulated a link between an austere Protestantism and the spirit, ethos or mentality of capitalism. According to Weber, ascetic Protestantism generated a new attitude towards embodiment and labour that was fundamental to the emergence of this new form of capitalism. Importantly, the process of rationalization emerged from within Christianity itself: impersonal rules and procedures supplanted magical and mystical notions and the body became an increasingly important site of disciplinary action. In a vision that would later be taken up by the writers of the Frankfurt School, Weber suggested that history was nothing other than the increasing subordination of the body-disciplined individual to rational-legal norms of authority through which social relations were increasingly instrumentalized and subject to the idea of the rational maximization of personal interest. These processes of rationalization and instrumentalization were central to the idea of dis-enchantment and indeed, at the close of *The Protestant Ethic*, Weber articulated a profoundly pessimistic vision of the future:

> The Puritan wanted to work in a calling; we are forced to do so. For when asceticism was carried out of the monastic cells into everyday life, and began to dominate worldly morality, it did its part in building the tremendous cosmos of the modern economic order. This order is now bound to the technical and economic conditions of machine production which today determine the lives of all the individuals who are born into this mechanism, not only those directly concerned with economic acquisition, with irresistible force. Perhaps it will so determine them until the last ton of fossilized coal is burnt. In Baxter's view the care for external goods should only lie on the shoulders of the 'saint like a light cloak, which can be thrown aside at any moment'. But fate decreed that the cloak should become an iron cage. (Weber 2002: 123)

This bleak vision of a disenchanted world was only mitigated by Weber's claim that irruptions of charisma – specifically the potency of religio-charismatic power – could break the bars of the iron cage:

Charisma in its most potent forms disrupts rational rule as well as tradition altogether and overturns all notions of sanctity. Instead of reverence for customs that are ancient and hence sacred, it enforces the inner subjection to the unprecedented and absolutely unique and therefore Divine. In this purely empirical and value-free sense charisma is indeed the specifically creative revolutionary force in history. (Weber 1978: 1117)

The narrative of modernity mapped out by Weber envisioned the increasing subordination of social life to the calculations of instrumental reason and posed the unfettered experience of charisma – short hand for a powerful religious experience – as the only potential source for creativity and liberation able to shatter the confines of the cage of instrumental rationality. This narrow view of reason on the one hand and of radical experience on the other refracted Nietzsche's interests in Greek tragedy and influenced Michel Foucault in his work on madness, psychiatry and the asylum. For both Nietzsche and Foucault, it was only

when the subject loses itself, when it sheers off from pragmatic experience in space and time, when it is stirred by the shock of the sudden ... [when] the norms of daily life have broken down, the illusions of habitual normality have collapsed – only then does the world of the unforeseen and the absolutely astonishing open up. (Habermas 1990: 93)

For Nietzsche, it would be art and performance – as explored in *The Birth of Tragedy* (1993) – that promised a way out from the constraints of Protestant, ascetic modernity. Similarly for Foucault, in the Preface to *History of Madness* (2006), it was as if there was something trying to escape from the confines of the total institution, for 'behind the psychiatrically engendered phenomenon of mental illness, and indeed behind the various masks of madness ... there is something authentic whose sealed mouth need only be opened up' (Habermas 1990: 240), such that Foucault could claim to have written 'a history not of psychiatry, but of madness itself, in all its vivacity, before it is captured by knowledge' with madness described as a 'wild state' and as a 'primitive purity' (Foucault 2006: xxxii–xxxiii).

The turbulent eddies of charisma and madness – in common with those of art and performance – have long been construed to have the potential to wrest the subject from itself, to renew it or to restore it or to completely transform it in much the same way that William James and Rudolf Otto imagined the contours of the paradigmatic religious experience, with its capacity to terrify and compel awe. Certainly too, the religious experience – the norm-transgressing experience – has provided certain avenues for thinking about religious and social change, but one that remains indelibly tied to the subject, and one incapable of understanding the complexities of change, its non-human dimensions and the tipping points and transitions between repertoires and between routine and improvisation.

A second set of resources for thinking about religious and social change derives from the works of Claude Lévi-Strauss and Mikhail Bakhtin respectively, specifically their concepts of *bricolage* and dialogism. *Bricolage* has been a handy concept for theorists of lived religion as it implies a level of improvised fabrication appropriate to the lived religion thesis. Danielle Kirby's suggestion that 'religious and spiritual *bricolage* is a common feature of contemporary religiosity' (2012: 39; italics in original) amounts to an orthodoxy of sorts in the lived religion milieu (see McGuire 2008). However, it is typically taken to mean individual choice, imagining individuals drawing from multiple sources for their identity, their religious narratives and their religio-cultural practices, which of course is not at all what Lévi-Strauss meant by the term (see Aupers and Houtman 2013: 174; Kirby 2012: 50–1). For Lévi-Strauss, *bricolage* was a mode of cognition characterized by the continuous re-cycling of a limited set of elements to produce, for example, new myths. The opposition drawn by

Lévi-Strauss between the *bricoleur* and the engineer is instructive: the engineer works from concepts to fulfil the objectives of specific projects; the *bricoleur* by contrast works with whatever comes to hand to generate order from the sensible qualities of things (Hénaff 1998: 141–58). Importantly, *bricolage* was never meant to be understood in terms of individual intentions or conceptions of authorship, but to denote a type of cognitive operation characteristic of certain cultures and societies.

Dialogism and linked notions of hybridity, intertextuality and heteroglossia have also proved useful to scholars interested in religious change, in particular for pinpointing instances of blending, mixing and creative borrowing in religious and religiously inflected forms of culture-making and production, including music (see Appert 2016; Hill 2017). James Cox (2017: 25) draws on Bakhtin as a means of theorizing religious change and creating a certain fusion, in Rainbow Spirit Theology, of indigenous Australian and Christian concepts and ideas. Cox uses Bakhtin precisely because it allows him to theorize Rainbow Spirit Theology in terms of 'will and intention' but also to position 'the indigenous participants in the creation of this new … [theology as] active, even subversive agents rather than passive victims acquiescing to the influences of an outside dominating force' (Cox 2017: 28). The centrality of political resistance to Cox's account is significant, but grounding change in intentional human action – whether framed in terms of *bricolage* or dialogism – means eliding a range of additional sources of agency and lines of causality. It is precisely these other lines and sources that are privileged in the account of the Cargo Cult assemblage that follows.

The Cargo Cult assemblage

At the end of the eighteenth century, when British Protestant missionary activity was expanding into new territories, and after the killing of Captain Cook in 1779 in Hawaii, the London Missionary Society made the region of Oceania, including Melanesia, a mission priority. But the missionaries who went to these places, according to MacCulloch (2010), often lacked a 'detailed grasp of Christian theology', although he suggests they did bring to the region 'charisma, a shrewd sense of what might appeal to local leaders in the Christian package and a determination to destroy the power of traditional cults' (2010: 876). Certainly, these missionaries disturbed local culture with their interventions and the new sources of power they and later colonial governments brought with them (for example, literacy, firearms and medicines). Conversion to Christianity was perhaps seen by locals as a means to access these new forms of power. Importantly, however, the interactions of Melanesian populations with Christianity was not a straightforward story of either conversion or resistance. Rather, these interactions were characterized by the emergence of local interpretations and Cargo Cults can be understood as arising in part from them.

It was not only Christianity that was brought to Melanesia. Colonial interventions drew the islands and their peoples into an emergent global economy and international politics. Papua was under German control from 1884 but, with the upheavals of World War I, changed hands to come under Australian jurisdiction. The Germans established vast plantations to export copra, which was used for making coconut oil. This did not change with the coming of the Australians, but the vagaries of global capitalism saw rapid shifts in the extractive colonial economy: by the 1930s, copra had been overtaken as the main export by rubber and gold. The labour for all of these enterprises was indentured: local men were signed up to work for a period of time (e.g., three years) during which time they lived in barracks, away from their villages. Mission, colonialism and exposure to the world capitalist economy constitute the complex, overlapping contexts in which the Cargo Cults emerged.

The Cargo Cults were very much the product of contact with European missionaries and colonizers. They were led by charismatic leaders who emerged from local populations, claiming that large quantities of cargo (trade goods brought into the islands by sea or by air) would arrive and be delivered to the locals to usher in the dawn of a new era of plenty in which the ancestors would return:

> Sometimes the word [cargo] meant money or various sorts of manufactured goods such as vehicles, packaged foods, refrigerators, guns, and tools. And sometimes, metaphorically, cargo represented the search for a new social and moral order that would ensure local sovereignty and the withdrawal of colonial rulers. In either case, people worked for and expected a sudden, miraculous transformation of their lives. Cargo cult prophets commonly drew on Christian millenarianism, sometimes conflating the arrival of cargo with Christ's second coming, often called 'Last Day'. (Lindstrom 2004: 15)

Central to the Cargo Cults was the concept of the 'end times' or 'end of days'. This concept was drawn from Christianity with its very particular temporal eschatology beginning with Eden, followed by the fall of humankind and then concluding with humanity's redemption through a final confrontation between good and evil understood as the 'end times'. However, the scholarship on Cargo Cults has stressed not only their religious dimensions but their political ones as well:

> 'Cargo Cult' is a name held to apply to any organized ritual activity characterized by a desire for 'cargo' based on existing religious beliefs. 'Cargo' in this context signifies not only the material goods of industrial production, but in general a higher standard of living and, most importantly, a status equal to that of the white colonizers ... The movements termed 'cargo cults' have also been called 'millenarian movements' ... or 'religious cults' ... 'social movements' ... 'crisis cults' ... 'forerunners of Melanesian nationalism' ... and 'millennial protest movements'. (Hermann 1992: 66)

The term 'Cargo Cult' also has a history, having first been used in the November 1945 edition of the magazine *Pacific Islands Monthly* (Lindstrom 2004: 19), while the first academic definition was developed by the anthropologist Lucy Mair, in 1948:

A notable feature of the reaction of the peoples of New Guinea to white rule is the occurrence at different times in almost every part of the Australian territories of a manifestation which used to be known as the 'Vailala Madness', but it is now more commonly described as the 'cargo cult' … The common characteristic is the insistence on the cargo of European goods to be sent by the ancestors, and the disappearance of the white man and his rule. Underlying the cargo myth is the idea that all trade goods have been manufactured in the spirit world by the ancestors as gifts for their descendants, and are misappropriated by white men. The prophet of one of these movements, who was named Batari, scored a strong point on one occasion when a crate marked 'battery' was unloaded from a ship – but not delivered to him. In every case, the leaders order native economic activities to be suspended. No gardens need be made, since the ancestors will provide all the food required – but only to those who have shown their faith by not growing any for themselves. For the same reason all the pigs are killed and eaten. The people spend their time preparing to welcome the ancestors; sometimes this involves special songs and dances. (Mair in Hermann 1992: 66–7)

The 'Vailala Madness' was first reported in 1919 in the villages of Nomu and Arihava in what was at the time designated the Gulf Division of Papua, and in what is today the southern coast of Papua New Guinea. The 'madness' was the first documented case of what would later be called a 'Cargo Cult'. Three features stand out in particular: (i) the idea that a steamer would arrive 'carrying the spirits of dead ancestors on board, who would bring with them the "Cargo"' (Williams 1977: 341–2; see also Worsley 1970: 91); (ii) the construction of various structures including buildings but also flagpoles said to be for communicating with the dead, and which were said by observers to imitate, in their style and construction, radio transmitters (Williams 1977: 349; see also Worsley 1970: 95) and (iii) bodily movements and actions performed by cultists (Williams 1977: 333–6; see also Worsley 1970: 85–6).

Francis Edgar Williams's essay 'The Vailala Madness and the Destruction of Native Ceremonies in the Gulf Division' (1977: 331–50) was originally published in 1923 and was composed from a variety of sources, including official reports, testimony from eye witnesses, as well as from observations and interviews conducted by Williams himself. It is notable not only as a more or less first-hand account of the events at Vailala but also for the tropes and metaphors through which Williams sought to make the events explicable to his white, colonial audience.

According to Williams, at the centre of the madness were psychological experiences and physical performances which he characterized in terms of psychological disturbance. By framing these experiences and performances in this way, the reader was more or less relieved of any obligation to try to understand them for they were placed by Williams in a secure interpretive room, beyond any need for understanding. As evidence of madness there was nothing for the anthropologist to understand: the experiences and performances were rendered religiously and socially meaningless.

As well as the language of madness and disturbance, Williams also deployed a language of epidemiology. That is, Williams encouraged his readers to imagine this madness as not merely the unfortunate affliction of a few, disturbed individuals, but as an epidemic sweeping through communities, causing considerable distress and disruption. The madness, then, was viral and contagious. Williams's use of registers of psychological disturbance and epidemiological contagion arguably lent his account a kind of aura of objectivity and, according to Andrew Lattas (1992a), this very much served the interests of the colonial government of the day:

Defining people as insane was a process of stripping from them any truth, any knowledge, any insight into their domination. Defining peoples as insane allowed the administration to dismiss people's criticisms of whites; those criticisms could now be viewed as another instance of their sickness, as part of their emotional instability. (Lattas 1992a: 3)

Conveniently, the language of madness and contagion separated the production of anthropological or scientific knowledge about the events at Vailala from the context of colonial domination (cf. Rosaldo 1986). Moreover, the language of madness and contagion was further enmeshed in racial stereotypes such as the idea that 'the native' was prone to 'lose command of himself and give way to excesses' (Williams 1977: 339). Yet, although Williams's account seemed to direct the reader, through apparently scientifically and objectively grounded references to psychiatry, epidemiology and race, to understand what happened at Vailala as an outbreak of something like mass hysteria, intriguingly, the account also provides a basis for an alternative interpretation based in ethnographic understanding of local cultural conceptions of death and the ancestors.

Firstly, of significance is the centrality of Christian elements, particularly those pertaining to the end times (Williams 1977: 344–5). Given the centrality of Christian millenarian expectations to Cargo Cults, why did 'the indigenous reception of Christianity repeatedly play up such images of dramatic transition at the expenses of other themes' (Kempf 1992: 73), or, to ask the question in another way, how do Melanesian cultures understand time and change, and why, in their encounter with Christianity, did they seize on the idea of the end times in particular? According to Kempf, Melanesian societies 'tend to give preference to an episodic or neo-episodic view of time, over a gradualist perspective' (1992: 79). The opposition between episodic and gradualist theories of time points to different understandings of change, one of which sees change as gradual, the other of which sees it as sudden and dramatic.

Kempf argues that Melanesian myths and rituals articulate an experience of time that is radical and dramatic rather than incremental or gradual. According to Kempf, this explains why Melanesian Christianity has had such a strong millennial emphasis.

Secondly, Williams reported that cultists believed that 'the ancestors, or more usually the deceased relatives, of the people were shortly to return to visit them' (1977: 341) by steamer and that these returning ancestors and relatives 'were expected to be white' (1977: 342). Indeed, white colonists were sometimes thought to be relatives of locals returned from the dead (contemporary white anthropologists have had similar experiences; see Leavitt 2000), while thirdly, central to the Cargo Cult was the concern with the dead and communication with them traditionally through offerings such as feasts, but later also through houses and flagpoles especially constructed for this purpose. The latter are particularly intriguing:

> There are certain individuals who can receive messages from the dead through its [the flagpole's] agency ... A trader on the coast was of opinion that the flag-poles were in the early days of the movement 'wirelesses intended for sending messages to the steamer'; and had even seen a pumpkin hoisted to the top of one of them with the apparent intention of despatching it to this destination. This explanation certainly squares with the method of 'receiving' described to me at Vailala; and there is to be seen at Opau, I am informed, a highly ingenious representation of an aerial, with wires of lawyer-cane, and a small office or cabin at either end for the operators. (Williams 1977: 348–9)

Williams regards the construction of these radios as an example of the 'preposterous beliefs' (1977: 331) of the cult. However, his account also opens up an entangled web of ideas fusing Christian and local cultural concerns about death and communication with the ancestors, the end of days, and with race and colonial politics. According to Lattas (2000), instead of regarding the radios constructed in the midst of the so-called Vailala madness as examples of some kind of primitive mentality, they can rather more productively be understood as attempts to address local concerns with the dead. Lattas argues that in 'cargo cults, the white man's mechanisms for revealing and tapping into concealed scientific forces was assimilated to Melanesian magical practices for revealing and tapping into the concealed forces belonging to the secluded world of the dead' (2000: 326). Cargo cultists sought to use the capacity of radio to bring distant spaces closer together, except these spaces pointed to a cosmic geography or spatiality, namely, the spaces of the living and the spaces of the ancestors. According to Lattas:

> Dreams, hallucinations, possession, and rituals were the customary practices of revelation ... used to redisclose and light up the world in different ways, namely from the standpoint of the dead. Borrowing and remaking these customary practices ... cult followers sought to end the isolation of the dead from the living by ... communicating with their ancestors via modern technology. (Lattas 2000: 326)

In short, cultists used methods borrowed from Western technology and applied them to the problem of communicating with the dead. But making the radios was not the only way in which Cargo Cultists tried to harness white experience:

> [C]argo cult leaders have often mimed European mannerisms: for example, European ways of walking in exaggerated steps with one's hands behind one's back; or European ways of talking, laughing or whistling; or European ways of writing and handling books. All of this is more than an appropriation of style; it uses style to appropriate the body image of the other and to capture the corporeal schemes and personhood of the other. The black man here

seeks to make himself into the double of the white man. He seeks to become white through occupying the corporeal regimes of the white man, that is by entering that space of movement and identity occupied by the white man's body ... Colonialism sought to make the black man into the double of the white man, but, along the way, state and church often lost control of this mimetic function and doubling process. In cargo cults, the process of borrowing the identity of the white man – the clothes, gestures, mannerisms and airs of the master – becomes part of a subversive culture. It becomes a magical rite designed to discover the bodily form which empowers the white man and to discover those secret rituals which the white man hides from the black man. (Lattas 1992b: 36)

Cargo Cults, then, were not confused mis-translations of Christian ideas about the end of days. Rather they were a complex blend of Melanesian conceptions of the dead and of communicating with the ancestors with Christian conceptions of the end times, entangled within the racialized and very political hierarchies of colonialism and capitalism and their technologies and practices of extraction:

The classic Western cargo cult stereotype emphasizes the disparity between indigenous magical, religious, cultural symbolic means, on the one hand, and European rational economic or political ends, on the other. The hallmarks of cargo cult include fits of hysterical shaking and frenzied activity involving the mimicking of European behaviours in ways that are quite apparently ineffectual in obtaining the goals attributed to them. Thus, 'cargo cult' stands for an intercultural misunderstanding. (Dalton 2004: 189–90)

As Peter Worsley argued, if Cargo Cults seemed irrational to Western observers like Edgar Williams, how did the whites appear to Melanesians, with their money, their steamers, their radios and their god?

[I]t is clear that the labelling of the cults as 'irrational' begs the question. Indeed, a Melanesian might make out a good case for flinging the label of 'madness' which has often been applied to these cults back at us, and asking whether his people, given the knowledge they possessed, have not made quite logical criticisms and interpretations of our own unpredictable and irrational society. (Worsley 1970: 46)

Perhaps rationality is less a universal yardstick for judging other cultures than a matter of contingent, historical and cultural perspective. Arguably, the Cargo Cults assemblage revealed an important similarity between Melanesian and Western cultures: desire for cargo or material goods through which to project personal status and power. Westerners represented Melanesians as 'confused people who use irrational means to pursue rational ends' (Otto 2004: 210), but surely they could have been accused of making the same mistake?

The Cargo Cult assemblage demonstrates religious and social change unfolding not according to any religious or secular teleology but in terms of the unexpected outcome of interactions among varied and contingent elements including a concatenation of objects and entities including missionaries, ancestors, radios, copra and embodied mannerisms all combining to generate something entirely unprecedented and new.

5

Towards a General Theory of Religion and Social Change

This book began by claiming that the secularization thesis and the lived religion thesis – the field's dominant theories of religious and social change – shared the same questionable foundation, namely, the rational choice-making, meaning-endowing, individual human subject. The question I posed was, what would an account of religious and social change look like if a non-, anti- or post-humanist point of departure was adopted instead? The proposal was to disrupt the sovereignty of the individual, human subject by situating it in a finely grained and thoroughly living, moving world of assemblages made up of contingent human and non-human interactants. I went on to propose a nomad science of religions as a means of taking the field to a new methodological and theoretical place.

Nomad science approaches reality 'as a set of flows rather than a series of discrete solids' with 'solids' understood as 'a special instance of flow' and as 'a temporary coagulation' (Adkins 2015: 197). For nomad science, the real is understood not in terms of any perfectly determinable world as was once imagined by the likes of Pierre-Simon Laplace, but in terms of unceasing movement unmoored from any substance, essence or being. A nomad science of religions, then, rejects both the teleology of modernity and secularization and the heroic powers of the subject and in their stead privileges movement and liveliness. It is a kind of methodological animism or fetishism for which change is unpredictable and open-ended.

David Chidester describes a debate in Turku, Finland in 1973 between Walter Capps and C. J. Bleeker. In the debate Bleeker urged his fellow scholars of religions to stick with philology and history, the tried and tested methods of the field. Capps, by contrast, insisted on the positionality of the scholar (Chidester 2018: 156) and on the necessity of experimentation with new theories and methods because 'only mobile theorizing ... [can] gain access to the dynamics of religion' (2018: 159). Capps was interested in change and for an approach to religions that privileged 'the moving, inconstant, spontaneous, irregular, [and] discontinuous' (Capps in Chidester 2018: 9) because

> Change is rugged and powerful. It transforms everything it touches. It rearranges boundaries. It upsets preestablished order. It modifies relationships. It alters contours. It reallocates and redistributes resources. It creates new shapes and inserts qualifications into definitions. Not content with simple composition, it decomposes, then recomposes. It modulates, transposes, transfigures, and diversifies. (Capps in Chidester 2018: 160–1)

Capps's interest in religious and social change was part and parcel of his work on the history of Christianity. There he identified two poles – one static and oriented towards preservation, the other dynamic and oriented towards the future – and saw their dialectic interplay as the key to understanding continuity and change in the tradition (2018: 162). Capps's envisioning of change in terms of the historical oscillations of a single binary opposition arguably functioned to stabilize and limit the circulation of elements at any given historical juncture to two oscillating clusters, spinning around two fixed, gravitational poles. Moreover, it was ultimately an oscillation of ideas closed to any conception of non-human agency and the role of things and objects in processes of change. Nevertheless, it is precisely Capps's interest in change that a nomad science of religions seeks to take forward. What, then, might a general, nomadic theory of religious and social change actually look like? I think it should include the following three, basic methodological procedures:

- methodological animism and fetishism: non-humans, including animals, plants, objects and things, participate with humans across a flat ontological plane of interactions in which neither humans nor non-humans are privileged;

- assemblages: interactions are shaped, stratified and spaced to form assemblages. Religions are assemblages formed from heterogeneous elements;

- change can be specified by empirically establishing and comparing the flows and patterns of differently located religious assemblages.

The animating principle of Deleuzian and Latourian ontological democracy offers a significant way forward to the question of religion and social change beyond both the secularization thesis and its rival, lived religion, as well as the arguably stale methodological debates about reductionism, phenomenology and explanation (see Stoddard 2018). However, the idea of a horizontal plane of interactants is probably a poor starting point for entertaining questions of power and inequality. As such, it is vital to add a dose of a Marx or a Haraway to the mix in order to draw out the extent to which interactions are asymmetrically entangled, just as a small drop of Lévi-Strauss allows for the sense that transformation does not necessarily come unexpectedly and catastrophically from without, but lies as a potential within any system, a point his work on myth – like his interest in music – bears out. It is to be hoped that others are interested enough to take up some of these ideas and put them to work.

Afterword: Assemblage Drawings

Atsuhide Ito

One day, I received a request from Paul for a set of drawings to illustrate his book. The drawings were to visualize the changing power configurations in the Philippines via Gilles Deleuze's concept of assemblages. The task of drawing made me think about lines and their relationship to drawing. The act of drawing a line, as simple as it sounds, causes a significant set of consequences. Drawing a line on a piece of paper divides a space into spaces and on a map the same act produces territories. The act of drawing structures a division and the consequence is territorialization. The simple act of drawing provokes a political consequence of division, territorialization and ownership.

On the contrary to the function of lines that divide, lines can also connect. Lines connect a point to another, establishing an alliance and a relationship and further alliances and relationships to be multiplied. Lines also link up with other lines while disrupting its extension, but stop and turn, changing their directions to reach another line, in a way to de-territorialize the already established structure of divisions and alliances. In so doing, the lines not only connect points and produce alliances, but also they can be met and crossed by chance, countering the forces aimed at an intended direction. Lines direct the mind of the viewer to travel from one point to another. For instance, a projectile thrown towards a target generates a curvilinear line representing the motion of the object. The potential point of impact is predicated as the projectile is thrown towards the target. That is to say, drawing is an assault. It is an act of directing thoughts and action towards a point at a given moment.

When tracing the projectile motion the line is a re-wind of motion as well as a fast-forward of potentiality. Like a genealogist linking the present to the past, or a historian speculatively identifying a cause of a present social situation, lines are a time-travel apparatus linking the present to the lost and forgotten points in the memories that are constructed as one traces thoughts through lines. They lead us into the past and provide potential passages into the future.

Lines also function to measure a length and duration. Through the process of measuring, lines make the observer compare and assess values in relation to the lines containing competing entities. For instance, in a swimming pool, swimmers compete by swimming in a rectangular area divided by equidistant lines. The architectural conception and construction of rectangles in a swimming pool is premised on a perception that space is isotropic: quality of space is the same everywhere. This allows production of spaces such as apartment blocks and multi-storey car parks. As Henri Lefebvre (1991) says, city planners and architects abstract, divide and produce spaces for the purposes of profit maximization and capital accumulation. According to Lefebvre, in the case of planning a multi-storey apartment building, the organic relations between the dweller and the place are severed; instead, the city planner and the architect abstract the space, and divide and multiply the abstracted space into multiple spaces for the purpose of capital accumulation.

In a drawing, lines are drawn to deny and negate the lines drawn previously, and even when erased, inscriptions are still visible: the traces of the drawing instrument, and the pressure the body of the artist placed on the paper. It is important to stress that the artist not only use the hand and press the drawing instrument onto the paper, but also the whole weight of the body is used to inscribe a mark. In this sense, the body of the artist becomes identical to the instrument: in short the body becomes a drawing machine.

All the above complexity is conveyed in the set of assemblage drawings in Chapter 3. In the first assemblage, power is concentrated in church squares. They appear rigid and static, and dwelled as an authority gathering forces into the concentrated squares despite them being colonial installations established in a relatively short period of time. These squares are connected through invisible lines to form a canalized network of power. Through this practice of concentrated centres of power and subservient terminal points within the network, the system produces a geographical hierarchy between centre and periphery. When drawn, such a system settles into a relatively figural landscape. Nonetheless it appears as a familiar topological landscape but simultaneously emerges as skeletonized power-scape, similar to the ways in which Arjun Appadurai (1996) outlines flows of power in the global network of distribution of media products and discourses.

The second assemblage observes a shift of power away from the town squares; the periphery gains intensity. The margins and edges of the rectangle of paper is more intensely worked and charcoal is smeared repeatedly in contrast to the centre of the image that is sparsely populated and left as traces instead of being an actively present locus. 'Intensity' is significant in Deleuze's writing as the body is not an organized system for Deleuze but it is an intensified materiality ready for affects. In drawing, intensity is un-representable but only presents itself through the process of the artist becoming a machine, a pure drawing machine who breathes in and out, weight on paper, stretching and contracting the body to inscribe. Then, how does the artist express and communicate a flow of movement? An arrow would be an obvious but a sign too literal. The use of an arrow would have reduced the drawing into one-dimensional illustration. Instead, I have used lines with thick ends, which look like a head of a line, to communicate a direction of movement. This has just kept the drawings to be on the side of 'asignifiying traits' (Deleuze 2005: 70). Deleuze defines the diagram as 'the operative set of traits and color patches, of lines and zones' (2005: 71), and yet he defines it with more details and says, 'it is indeed a chaos, a catastrophe, but also a germ of order or rhythm. It is a violent chaos in relation to the figurative givens, but it is a germ of rhythm' (ibid.). I was pressing hard on cotton-like paper to leave definite traces of my thinking. Sometimes I was responding and more precisely reacting to the marks that I had previously made. It was more accurate to describe it as a violent, obsessive and séance-like engagement with the materiality of the image unfolding in front of me. In this trance-like chrono-topos of drawing I was treading on the border of 'the collapse of visual coordinates' (ibid.), sometimes holding myself as an organizer of marks, and other times being lost in the sensations in the seeming chaos. As a result the drawings were always at the point of near collapse, but I was holding them within a diagrammatic and figural structure. The drawings encounter regularly a breaking point but they are pulled back to remain structurally diagrammatic and figural. As opposed to Deleuze's perception of work as a catastrophe, none of the breaking points are a singular catastrophe, but holding on to the structure of image right on the border of implosion.

In the third assemblage, forces explode from the periphery as a new centre. Power is dispersed and flies out into polyvalent directions that affect the atmosphere. Pictorially, the old centre square from which power once flowed appears caved in. If talking about the body, it resembles a great anus or gaping mouth in the act of sucking or spitting. Diagrammatically, the explosive sucking and spitting of power renders the traditional squares of power insignificant.

Marks are no longer grounded but float in the indefinable spaces in the fourth assemblage. The lines branch out as often as they cross over, link up or clash against one another. Some areas appear as more intense than other dots, spots and stains. They are forging spontaneous alliances to structure a system but they are simultaneously decomposing themselves before becoming a system. Hierarchy is constructed though it is no longer a vertical one, only visible as concentration of power and de-concentration, while each element averts against the systemic structure and flees from the gravitational and topological structuring. The viewer of the drawing is tasked an apophenic exercise to decipher patterns in the structuring and de-structuring, thus un-structuring fragments that are short of producing a system. Drawing for an artist is this task of letting the undetectable structuring of power appear in the domain of visibility. Hito Steyerl (2017) discusses how apophenia, an ability to perceive patterns in background noise, is a skill that helps us see beyond the façade of reality organized through electronic networks of pulses and data. In a network society, marks are no longer located in the pictorial scheme organized according to geographical coordinates, or the division between the celestial and the ground.

Deleuze's notion of assemblage, when referring to the drawings, is a snapshot of a configuration of power at a given moment. Different from Gerald Raunig's (2010) reading of machinic assemblage as a concatenation of social resistance and a formation of inventive alliances, I stay with the specific reference to the drawings that the changing configurations of power are framed like a snapshot at a given moment. How Deleuze explains the diagram in his book about Francis Bacon provides some guidance. To follow his notion of diagram assemblage is a configuration of forces in a synchronic diagram. It is a film still that captures invisible power struggles. Of course, Deleuze does not mean that the diagram is an illustration in the sense of an annotative aid. A diagram does not serve ideas, but it itself is an idea in its image and its materiality. Appadurai's notion of flow is useful here as power and influences are dispersed and acquired, adopted and deployed. However, different from the notion of flow, the assemblage through Tremlett's looking-glass includes struggles and flights rather than the flows that are organized through relatively established networks. To visualize a configuration of power, the artist attempts to map out movements of forces in a power struggle.

In effect the outcome is a skeletonized power-scape, that captures emerging flows but also clashes of power. Suffice to mention Jacques Lacan's (1977) discussion of the phallus in which power is not held by an authorial agent but in terms of relational forces that are played out, negotiated, imposed and resisted. In other words, it is constantly changing shape, intensity, speed, direction and impact. In the assemblage drawings I did not intend to capture them but imagine them through Tremlett's writing and let them materially emerge in the form of drawing. When drawing is understood as a form of hunting a prey, as Thomas Zummer (2012) suggests, in the act of drawing, the artist attempts to capture a scene, or a figure. For instance, a drawing of a figure in motion becomes an exercise of capturing the figure in motion. In this sense drawing is an act of the hunter throwing a lasso around an animal-other. Consequently the drawing attempts to captivate and arrest the viewer. The act of drawing as hunting and a piece of drawing as a catch seems fitting but, at the same time, the metaphor conceals the artist-hunter's presence in the close encounter with the prey as the viewer focuses on the captured. When the event of drawing is an act of capture the artist-hunter in fact stands proximal to the prey. Similarly both Deleuze and Tremlett participate in the historical process of territorialization, de-territorialization and re-territorialization with their analysis of power. For my part, while carrying out the task of drawing I have attempted to produce images of power by relying on lines as my weapon of choice – although, perhaps, 'weapon' is an exaggeration even when a drawing is thought of as a visual assault on the senses. By adopting Zummer's metaphor of drawing as an act of hunting a prey, mistakenly I would be suggesting knowledge as animal-other –that is, the shifting power-scape, ready to be captured. Instead, to reflect more sincerely on my experience of making assemblage drawings, I was trapped in the unknowingness like a prey since the request for the drawings was made. In the process, I have gone through technical frustrations when I was not able to see what I wanted to see when drawing, and also had delightful moments when accidental marks led to surprising results. In this particular sense, drawing as much as assemblage is a production of knowledge out of un-knowingness, an attempt to see more than one is routinely possible to see, and grasp the imperceptible configurations of power.

NOTES

Introduction

1 It is important to note that prior to the arrival of Spain, the Philippines was entangled within a number of networks and flows. From as far back as the seventh century CE such networks and flows included trade with the Arab and Indian worlds; from the twelfth-century, migrations of Borneo Malays to Manila and Chinese and Arab traders and missionaries to Sulu; while in the sixteenth century the Visayan port of Cebu traded items from Mindanao, Japan and China (see Francisco 2018: 254).

Chapter 1

1 'Plutôt qu'anthropologie, il faudrait écrire "entropologie" le nom d'une discipline vouée à étudier dans ses manifestations les plus hautes ce proccessus de désintégration' (Lévi-Strauss 1955: 496).

2 Anna Feigenbaum (2014) details a trial around Occupy Fort Meyers in America where the Court ruled that while 'fake sleeping' was 'an acceptable mode of communicative protest ... real sleeping was not' (Feigenbaum 2014: 19). The Fort Meyers camp had been established in the city's park. While protest with a tent in the park was legal, actually using the tent for the purposes of sleeping, was not!

3 Activists describe 'pre-figurative politics' as a form of political association, action or structuring that anticipates the kind of society that they want to create (see Graeber 2013).

4 Many of the speeches and discussions were recorded by activists themselves and used to be accessible at http://occupydemocracy.org.uk/.

Chapter 2

1 It is notable that vitalism's implication in conceptions of race and the fascist and Nazi politics of pre-war Germany and Europe more widely has been frequently elided, despite the forensic investigations of Harrington (1996) and Jones (2010).

2 Dennett's approach is the mirror-image of the early twentieth-century German philosopher Ludwig Klages, who compared 'human rationality to a parasite that had worked across history to asphyxiate the originally intuitive and prophetic soul of primeval humanity' (Harrington 1996: 32).

Chapter 3

1 More recent studies interested in animistic conceptions of power and objects with unusual qualities have made use of Latourian ideas about object-agency. See the excellent volume of essays edited by Kirsten Endres and Andrea Lauser (2011).

2 Urbanization is typically conceptualized in secular and developmental terms but, as the Global Challenges research project 'Religious Urbanisation and Infrastructural Lives in African Mega-Cities' led by David Garbin, Simon Coleman and Gareth Millington makes clear, urban and developmental imaginaries are also articulated through religions and by religious actors. See rua-project.ac.uk.

REFERENCES

Adkins, B. (2015), *Deleuze and Guattari's* A Thousand Plateaus: *A Critical Introduction and Guide*, Edinburgh: Edinburgh University Press.

Albinus, L. (2008), 'Dangerous Ideas: The Spell of *Breaking the Spell*', *Method and Theory in the Study of Religion*, 20 (1): 22–35.

Althusser, L. (2005), *For Marx*, translated by B. Brewster, London: Verso.

Ammerman, N. (2007), 'Introduction: Observing Modern Religious Lives', in N. Ammerman (ed.), *Everyday Religion: Observing Modern Religious Lives*, 3–20, Oxford: Oxford University Press.

Andaya, L. Y. (1999), 'Interactions with the Outside World and Adaptation in Southeast Asian Society, 1500–1800', in N. Tarling (ed.), *The Cambridge History of Southeast Asia Volume II: From c. 1500 to c. 1800*, 1–57, Cambridge: Cambridge University Press.

Anderson, B. (1972), 'The Idea of Power in Javanese Culture', in C. Holt (ed.), *Culture and Politics in Indonesia*, 1–70, Ithaca, NY: Cornell University Press.

Anderson, B. (2016), *Imagined Communities: Reflections on the Origin and Spread of Nationalism*, revised edn, London: Verso.

Appadurai, A. (1986), 'Introduction: Commodities and the Politics of Value', in A. Appadurai (ed.), *The Social Life of Things*: *Commodities in Cultural Perspective*, 1–63, Cambridge: Cambridge University Press.

Appadurai, A. (1996), *Modernity at Large: Cultural Dimensions of Globalization*, Minneapolis: University of Minnesota Press.

Appert, C. M. (2016), 'On Hybridity in African Popular Music: The Case of Senegalese Hip Hop', *Ethnomusicology*, 60 (2): 279–99.

Asad, T. (1993), *Genealogies of Religion: Discipline and Reasons of Power in Christianity and Islam*, Baltimore: The Johns Hopkins University Press.

Atran, S. and J. Henrich (2010), 'The Evolution of Religion: How Cognitive By-Products, Adaptive Learning Heuristics, Ritual Displays and Group Competition Generate Deep Commitments to Prosocial Religions', *Biological Theory*, 5 (1): 18–30.

Aupers, S. and D. Houtman (2013), 'Beyond the Spiritual Supermarket: The Social and Public Significance of New Age Spirituality', in S. J. Sutcliffe and I. S. Gilhus (eds), *New Age Spirituality: Rethinking Religion*, 174–96, Durham: Acumen.

Badcock, A. and R. Johnston (2009), 'Placemaking through Protest: An Archaeology of the Lees Cross and Endcliffe Protest Camp, Derbyshire, England', *Archaeologies: Journal of the World Archaeological Congress*, 5 (2): 306–22.

Badia, L. (2016), 'Theorizing the Social: Emile Durkheim's Theory of Force and Energy', *Cultural Studies*, 36 (6): 969–1000.

Bailey, E. (1998), *Implicit Religion: An Introduction*, London: Middlesex University Press.

Ball, P. (2004), *Critical Mass: How One Thing Leads to Another*, London: Arrow Books.

Barrett, J. (2011), 'Cognitive Science of Religion: Looking Back, Looking Forward', *Journal for the Scientific Study of Religion*, 50 (2): 229–39.

Barthes, R. (1977), 'The Death of the Author', in *Image Music Text*, translated by S. Heath, 142–48. London: Fontana Press.

Baudrillard, J. (2007), *In the Shadow of the Silent Majorities*, translated by P. Foss, J. Johnston, P. Patton and A. Berardini, Introduction, S. Lotringer, C. Kraus and H. El Kholti. Los Angeles: Semiotext(e).

Bauman, Z. (1999), *Culture as Praxis*, London: Sage.

Bauman, Z. (2000), *Liquid Modernity*, Cambridge: Polity.

Bauman, Z. (2005), 'Durkheim's Society Revisited', in J. C. Alexander and P. Smith (eds), *The Cambridge Companion to Durkheim*, 360–82, Cambridge: Cambridge University Press.

Bennett, J. (2010), *Vibrant Matter: A Political Ecology of Things*, Durham, NC: Duke University Press.

Berger, P. L. (2014), *The Many Altars of Modernity: Toward a Paradigm for Religion in a Pluralist Age*, Berlin: de Gruyter.

Bering, J. (2003), 'Towards a Cognitive Theory of Existential Meaning', *New Ideas in Psychology*, 21: 101–20.

Berking, H., S. Steets and J. Schwenk, eds (2018), *Religious Pluralism and the City: Inquiries into Postsecular Urbanism*, London: Bloomsbury.

Best, S. and D. Kellner (1991), *Postmodern Theory: Critical Interrogations*, London: Macmillan.

Bloch, M. (1977), 'The Past and the Present in the Present', *Man*, 12 (2): 278–92.

Bogard, W. (1987), 'Sociology in the Absence of the Social: The Significance of Baudrillard for Contemporary Thought', *Philosophy and Social Criticism*, 13 (3): 227–42.

Bolasco, M. V. (1994a), 'Marxists and Churchmen', in E. de la Torre (ed.), *Points of Departure: Essays on Christianity, Power and Social Change*, 235–55, Manila: St. Scholastica's College.

Bolasco, M. V. (1994b), 'Harmony and Contradiction: The Marxist-Christian Dialogue since the Christians for National Liberation', in E. de la Torre (ed.), *Points of Departure: Essays on Christianity, Power and Social Change*, 256–69, Manila: St. Scholastica's College.

Bowler, P. J. (2009), *Evolution: The History of an Idea*, 25th edn, Berkeley and London: University of California Press.

Boyer, P. (1992), 'Explaining Religious Ideas: Elements of a Cognitive Approach', *NUMEN*, 39 (1): 25–57.

Boyer, P. (2000), *Religion Explained: The Evolutionary Origins of Religious Thought*, New York: Basic Books.

Boyer, P. (2003), 'Religious Thought and Behaviour as By-Products of Brain Function', *Trends in Cognitive Science*, 7 (3): 119–24.

Bruce, S. (2002), *God is Dead: Secularization in the West*, Oxford: Blackwell.

Bulloch, H. C. M. (2017), *In Pursuit of Progress: Narratives of Development on a Philippine Island*, Honolulu: University of Hawaii Press.

Burrow, J. W. (1968), *Evolution and Society: A Study in Victorian Social Theory*, Cambridge: Cambridge University Press.

Callinicos, A. (1999), *Social Theory: An Historical Introduction*, Cambridge: Polity Press.

Cannell, F. (2006), 'Introduction: The Anthropology of Christianity', in F. Cannell (ed.), *The Anthropology of Christianity*, 1–50, Durham, NC: Duke University Press.

Castells, M. (2000), 'Toward a Sociology of the Network Society', *Contemporary Sociology*, 29 (5): 693–99.

Castells, M. (2012), *Networks of Outrage and Hope: Social Movements in the Internet Age*, Cambridge: Polity.

Cave, D. (1993), *Mircea Eliade's Vision for a New Humanism*, Oxford: Oxford University Press.

Chandler, D. (2007), 'The Possibilities of Post-Territorial Political Community', *Area*, 39 (1): 116–19.

Chen, K.-H. (1987), 'The Masses and the Media: Baudrillard's Implosive Postmodernism', *Theory, Culture and Society*, 4 (1): 71–88.

Chidester, D. (2018), *Religion: Material Dynamics*, Oakland, CA: University of California Press.

Choay, F. (1997), *The Rule and the Model: On the Theory of Architecture and Urbanism*, Cambridge, MA: MIT Press.

Clastres, P. (1994), *The Archeology of Violence*, translated by J. Herman, New York: Semiotext(e).

Claussen, H. L. (2001), *Unconventional Sisterhood: Feminist Catholic Nuns in the Philippines*, Ann Arbor: The University of Michigan Press.

Clifford, J. (1983), 'On Ethnographic Authority', *Representations*, 2: 118–46.

Coggins, O. (2018), *Mysticism, Ritual and Religion in Drone Metal*, London: Bloomsbury.

Cole, S. (2003), 'Appropriated Meanings: Megaliths and Tourism in Eastern Indonesia', *Indonesia and the Malay World*, 31 (89): 140–51.

Cole, S. (2007), 'Beyond Authenticity and Commodification', *Annals of Tourism Research*, 34 (4): 943–60.

Collier, S. J. and A. Ong (2005), 'Global Assemblages, Anthropological Problems', in Aihwa Ong and Stephen J. Collier (eds), *Global Assemblages: Technology, Politics, and Ethics as Anthropological Problems*, 3–21, Oxford: Blackwell.

Comte, A. (1998), 'Philosophical Considerations on the Sciences and Scientists', in H. S. Jones (ed.), *Comte: Early Political Writings*, 145–86, Cambridge: Cambridge University Press.

Connell, J. (1999), 'Beyond Manila: Walls, Malls and Private Spaces', *Environment and Planning*, 31 (3): 417–39.

Connerton, P. (1989), *How Societies Remember*, Cambridge: Cambridge University Press.

Conway, J. M., M. Osterweil and E. Thorburn (2018), 'Theorising Power, Difference and the Politics of Social Change: Problems and Possibilities in Assemblage Thinking', *Studies in Social Justice*, 12 (1): 1–18.

Corning, P. A. (2012), 'The Re-emergence of Emergence, and the Causal Role of Synergy in Emergent Evolution', *Synthese*, 185: 295–317.

Cox, J. (2006), *A Guide to the Phenomenology of Religion: Key Figures, Formative Influences and Subsequent Debates*, London: Continuum.

Cox, J. (2017), 'The Debate between E. B. Tylor and Andrew Lang over the Theory of Primitive Monotheism: Implications for Contemporary Studies of Indigenous Religions', in P.-F. Tremlett, L. T. Sutherland and G. Harvey (eds), *Edward Burnett Tylor, Religion and Culture*, 11–28, London: Bloomsbury.

Dalton, D. (2004), 'Cargo and Cult: The Mimetic Critique of Capitalist Culture', in H. Jebens (ed.), *Cargo, Cult and Culture Critique*, 187–208, Honolulu: University of Hawaii Press.

Darwin, C. (2008 [1859]), *On the Origin of Species*, Oxford: Oxford University Press.

Davidman, L. (2007), 'The New Voluntarism and the Case of Unsynagogued Jews', in N. Ammerman (ed.), *Everyday Religion: Observing Modern Religious Lives*, 51–67, Oxford: Oxford University Press.

Dawkins, R. (2007), *The God Delusion*, London: Black Swan.

DeLanda, M. (2011), *Philosophy and Simulation: The Emergence of Synthetic Reason*, London: Bloomsbury.

DeLanda, M. (2016), *Assemblage Theory*, Edinburgh: Edinburgh University Press.

Deleuze, G. (2005), *Francis Bacon: The Logic of Sensation*, translated by D. W. Smith, London: Bloomsbury.

Deleuze, G. and F. Guattari (2014), *A Thousand Plateaus: Capitalism and Schizophrenia*, translated by B. Massumi, London: Bloomsbury.

Dennett, D. C. (2006), *Breaking the Spell: Religion as a Natural Phenomenon*, London: Penguin.

Derrida, J. (1997), *Of Grammatology*, translated by G. C. Spivak. Baltimore: Johns Hopkins University Press.

Dubuisson, D. (2006), *Twentieth Century Mythologies: Dumézil, Lévi-Strauss, Eliade*, translated by M. Cunningham, 2nd edn, London: Equinox.

Durkheim, E. (1915), *The Elementary Forms of the Religious Life*, translated by J. W. Swain, London: Allen and Unwin.

Durkheim, E. (1952), *Suicide: A Study in Sociology*, translated by J. A. Spaulding and G. Simpson. London: Routledge.

Durkheim, E. (1960a), *Les Formes Elémentaires de la Vie Religieuse: Le Système Totémique en Australie*, Paris: PUF.

Durkheim, E. (1960b), 'The Dualism of Human Nature and its Social Conditions', in K. H. Wolff (ed.), *Emile Durkheim 1858–1917*, translated by C. Blend, 325–40, Ohio: Ohio State University Press.

Durkheim, E. (2013), *De la Division du Travail*, Paris: Quadrige.

Durkheim, E. (2014), *The Division of Labor in Society*, edited by S. Lukes, translated by W. D. Halls, New York: Free Press.

Edwards, J. (2003), 'Evolutionary Psychology and Politics', *Economy and Society*, 32 (2): 280–98.

Eisentadt, S. N. (2000), 'Multiple Modernities', *Daedalus*, 29 (1): 1–29.

Eliade, M. (1959), *The Sacred and the Profane: The Nature of Religion*, translated by W. R. Trask, New York: Harvest.

Eliade, M. (1969a), 'Crisis and Renewal', in idem, *The Quest: History and Meaning in Religion*, 54–71, Chicago: University of Chicago Press.

Eliade, M. (1969b), 'Preface', in idem, *The Quest: History and Meaning in Religion*, Chicago: University of Chicago Press.

Eliade, M. (1969c), 'The New Humanism', in idem, *The Quest: History and Meaning in Religion*, 1–11, Chicago: University of Chicago Press.

Endres, K. W. and A. Lauser (2011), *Engaging the Spirit World: Popular Beliefs and Practices in Modern Southeast Asia*, New York: Berghahn Books.

Evans-Pritchard, E. E. (1940), *The Nuer: A Description of the Modes of Livelihood and Political Institutions of a Nilotic People*, Oxford: Clarendon Press.

Feigenbaum, A. (2014), 'Resistant Matters: Tents, Tear Gas and the "Other Media" of Occupy', *Communication and Critical/Cultural Studies*, 11 (1): 15–24.

Feyerabend, P. (2010), *Against Method: Outline of an Anarchist Theory of Knowledge*, 4th edn, London: Verso.

Fish, J. S. (2002), 'Religion and the Changing Intensity of Emotional Solidarities in Durkheim's *The Division of Labour in Society* (1893)', *Journal of Classical Sociology*, 2 (2): 203–23.

Fitzgerald, T. (2000), *The Ideology of Religious Studies*, Oxford: Oxford University Press.

Fitzgerald, T. (2003), 'Playing Language Games and Performing Rituals: Religious Studies as Ideological State Apparatus', *Method and Theory in the Study of Religion*, 15 (3): 209–54.

Flood, C. and G. Grindon (2014), *Disobedient Objects*, London: V and A Publishing.

Foronda, M. A. (1961), *Cults Honouring Rizal*, Manila: De la Salle College.

Foucault, M. (1970), *The Order of Things: An Archaeology of the Human Sciences*, London: Routledge.

Foucault, M. (1991), *Discipline and Punish: The Birth of the Prison*, London: Penguin.

Foucault, M. (2004), *Society Must be Defended: Lectures at the Collège de France, 1975–76*, London: Penguin.

Foucault, M. (2006), *History of Madness*, translated by J. Murphy and J. Khalfa, London: Routledge.

Francisco, J. M. C. (2010), 'Mapping Religious and Civil Spaces in Traditional and Charismatic Christianities in the Philippines', *Philippine Studies*, 58 (1-2): 185–221.

Francisco, J. M. C. (2018), 'Hybridity in Asian Christian Discourse: Critical Issues from Asian Christian Experience', *International Journal of Asian Christianity*, 1 (2): 250–68.

Frank, J. (2006), 'Thinkers and Liars', *The New Republic*, 30 November: 31–37.

Franklin, A. (2017), 'The More-Than-Human City', *The Sociological Review*, 65 (2): 202–17.

Frazer, J. G. (1900), 'Preface to the Second Edition', in idem, *The Golden Bough: A Study in Magic and Religion*, 2nd edn, London: Macmillan and Co.

Frazer, J. G. (1910), *Totemism and Exogamy: A Treatise on Certain Early Forms of Superstition and Society Volume 1*, London: Macmillan and Co.

Frazer, J. G. (1931), 'The Scope and Method of Mental Anthropology', in idem, *Garnered Sheaves: Essays, Addresses, and Reviews*, 234–51, New York: Freeport.

Frichot, H., C. Gabrielsson and J. Metzger, eds (2016), *Deleuze and the City*, Edinburgh: Edinburgh University Press.

Gane, M. (1991), *Baudrillard: Critical and Fatal Theory*, London: Routledge.

Garbin, D. and A. Strhan, eds (2017), *Religion and the Global City*, London: Bloomsbury.

Gariguez, E. A. (2008), 'Articulating Mangyan-Alangans' Indigenous Ecological Spirituality as Paradigm for Sustainable Development and Well-Being', unpublished PhD diss., Asian Social Institute.

Geertz, C. (1973), 'Thick Description: Toward an Interpretive Theory of Culture', in idem, *The Interpretation of Cultures: Selected Essays*, 3–32, New York: Basic Books.

Geertz, C. (1983), 'Blurred Genres: The Refiguration of Social Thought', in idem, *Local Knowledge: Further Essays in Interpretive Anthropology*, 19–35, New York: Basic Books.

Gilhus, I. S. and S. J. Sutcliffe (2013), 'Conclusion: New Age Spiritualities – "Good to Think" in the Study of Religion', in S. J. Sutcliffe and I. S. Gilhus (eds), *New Age Spirituality: Rethinking Religion*, 256–62, Durham: Acumen.

Gilmore, J., W. Jackson and H. Monk (2016), *Keep Moving: Report on the Policing of the Barton Moss Community Protection Camp November 2013 – April 2014*, Liverpool: Centre for the Study of Crime, Criminalisation and Social Exclusion, Liverpool John Moores University and the Centre for URBan Research (CURB), University of York.

Giordano, P. T. (1988), *Awakening to Mission: The Philippine Catholic Church 1965–1981*, Manila: New Day Publishers.

González, G. (2015), *Shape-Shifting Capital: Spiritual Management, Critical Theory, and the Ethnographic Project*, Lanham, MD: Lexington Books.

Gorospe, V. R. (1992), *Banahaw: Conversations with a Pilgrim to the Power Mountain*, Manila: Bookmark.

Graeber, D. (2007), 'On the Phenomenology of Giant Puppets: Broken Windows, Imaginary Jars of Urine, and the Cosmological Role of the Police in American Culture', in idem, *Possibilities: Essays on Hierarchy, Rebellion and Desire*, 375–417, Oakland, CA: AK Press.

Graeber, D. (2013), *The Democracy Project: A History. A Crisis. A Movement*, London: Allen Lane.

Graeber, D. (2014a), 'Occupy Democracy is Not Considered Newsworthy: It Should Be', *The Guardian*, 27 October.

Graeber, D. (2014b), *Debt: The First 5,000 Years*, New York: Melville House.

Grindon, G. (2007), 'The Breath of the Possible', in S. Shukaitis, D. Graeber with E. Biddle (eds), *Constituent Imagination: Militant Investigations, Collective Theorization*, 94–107, Oakland, CA: AK Press.

Grondin, J. (1994), *Introduction to Philosophical Hermeneutics*, New Haven, CT: Yale University Press.

Groot, K. de (2006), 'The Church in Liquid Modernity: A Sociological and Theological Exploration of a Liquid Church', *International Journal for the Study of the Christian Church*, 6 (1): 91–103.

Groot, K. de (2008), 'Three Types of Liquid Religion', *Implicit Religion*, 11 (3): 277–96.

Guan, A. C. (2018), *Southeast Asia's Cold War: An Interpretive History*, Honolulu: University of Hawaii Press.

Guthrie, S. (2013), 'Early Cognitive Theories of Religion: Robin Horton and his Predecessors', in D. Xygalatas and W. W. McCorkle (eds), *Mental Culture: Classical Social Theory and the Cognitive Science of Religion*, 35–51, Durham: Acumen.

Habermas, J. (1990), *The Philosophical Discourse on Modernity*, translated by Frederik Lawrence, Cambridge: Polity Press.

Hall, S. (1983), 'The Problem of Ideology: Marxism without Guarantees', in B. Matthews (ed.), *Marx: 100 Years On*, 57–86, London: Lawrence and Wishart.

Hamilton-Paterson, J. (1999), *America's Boy: A Century of Colonialism in the Philippines*, London: Granta Books.

Haraway, D. (1991a), 'Situated Knowledges: The Science Question in Feminism and the Privilege of Partial Perspective', in idem, *Simians, Cyborgs and Women: The Reinvention of Nature*, 183–201, London: Free Association Books.

Haraway, D. (1991b), 'A Cyborg Manifesto: Science, Technology, and Socialist Feminism in the Late Twentieth Century', in idem, *Simians, Cyborgs and Women: The Reinvention of Nature*, 149–81, London: Free Association Books.

Haraway, D. (2018), 'Gene: Maps and Portraits of Life Itself', in idem, *Modest_Witness @ Second Millennium. FemaleMan_Meets_OncoMouse: Feminism and Technoscience*, 131–72, 2nd edn, London: Routledge.

Harding, S. G. (2004), 'A Socially Relevant Philosophy of Science? Resources from Standpoint Theory's Controversality', *Hypatia: A Journal of Feminist Philosophy*, 19 (1): 25–47.

Harman, G. (2018), *Object-Oriented Ontology: A New Theory of Everything*, London: Pelican.

Harrington, A. (1996), *Reenchanted Science: Holism in German Culture from Wilhelm II to Hitler*, Princeton, NJ: Princeton University Press.

Harrison, R. (2013), *Heritage: Critical Approaches*, London: Routledge.

Harvey, D. (1990), *The Condition of Postmodernity: An Enquiry into the Origins of Cultural Change*, Oxford: Blackwell.

Harvey, G. (2013), *Food, Sex and Strangers: Understanding Religion as Everyday Life*, Durham: Acumen.

Hawkes, T. (1983), *Structuralism and Semiotics*, London: Methuen and Co.

Heelas, P. (2008), *Spiritualities of Life: New Age Romanticism and Consumptive Capitalism*, Oxford: Blackwell.

Heine-Geldern, R. (2006), 'State and Kingship in Southeast Asia', in D. R. SarDesai (ed.), *Southeast Asian History: Essential Readings*, 46–63, Cambridge, MA: Westview Press.

Hénaff, M. (1998), *Claude Lévi-Strauss and the Making of Structural Anthropology*, translated by M. Baker, Minneapolis: University of Minnesota Press.

Hermann, E. (1992) 'The Yali Movement in Retrospect: Rewriting History, Redefining Cargo Cult', *Oceania*, 63 (1): 55–71.

Hill, J. (2017), 'A Mystical Cosmopolitanism: Sufi Hip Hop and the Aesthetics of Islam in Dakar', *Culture and Religion*, 18 (4): 388–408.

Holman, P. (2010), *Engaging Emergence: Turning Upheaval into Opportunity*, Oakland, CA: Berrett-Koehler Publishers.

Ileto, R. C. (1998a), 'Rural Life in a Time of Revolution', in idem, *Filipinos and Their Revolution: Event, Discourse, and Historiography*, 79–98, Manila: Ateneo de Manila University Press.

Ileto, R. C. (1998b), 'Rizal and the Underside of Philippine History', in idem, *Filipinos and Their Revolution: Event, Discourse, and Historiography*, 29–78, Manila: Ateneo de Manila University Press.

Ileto, R. C. (1999), 'Religion and Anti-Colonial Movements', in N. Tarling (ed.), *The Cambridge History of Southeast Asia Volume III: From c. 1800 to the 1930s*, 193–244, Cambridge: Cambridge University Press.

Ileto, R. C. (2011), *Pasyon and Revolution: Popular Movements in the Philippines, 1840–1910*, 8th edn, Manila: Ateneo de Manila University Press.

Ingold, T. (1986), *Evolution and Social Life*, Cambridge: Cambridge University Press.

Ingold, T. (1995), 'Building, Dwelling, Living: How Animals and People Make Themselves at Home and in the World', in M. Strathern (ed.), *Shifting Contexts: Transformations in Anthropological Knowledge*, 57–80, London: Routledge.

Ingold, T. (2001), 'From Complementarity to Obviation: On Dissolving the Boundaries between Social and Biological Anthropology, Archaeology, and Psychology', in S. Oyama, E. Griffiths and R. D. Gray (eds), *Cycles of Contingency: Developmental Systems and Evolution*, 255–80, Cambridge, MA: MIT Press.

Ingold, T. (2007a), 'The Trouble with "Evolutionary Biology"', *Anthropology Today*, 23 (2): 13–17.

Ingold, T. (2007b), *Lines: A Brief History*, London: Routledge.

Jameson, F. (1972), *The Prison-House of Language: A Critical Account of Structuralism and Russian Formalism*, Princeton, NJ: Princeton University Press.

Jenks, C. (2003), *Transgression*, London: Routledge.

Johnson, C. (2003), *Claude Lévi-Strauss: The Formative Years*, Cambridge: Cambridge University Press.

Jones, D. V. (2010), *The Racial Discourses of Life Philosophy: Négritude, Vitalism and Modernity*, New York: Columbia University Press.

Jong, J. (2017), '"Belief in Spiritual Beings": E. B. Tylor's (Primitive) Cognitive Theory of Religion', in P.-F. Tremlett, L. T. Sutherland and G. Harvey (eds), *Edward Burnett Tylor, Religion and Culture*, 47–61, London: Bloomsbury.

Kataoka, T. (2012), 'Introduction: De-Institutionalising Religion in Southeast Asia', *Southeast Asian Studies*, 1 (3): 361–63.

Kempf, W. (1992), '"The Second Coming of the Lord": Early Christianisation, Episodic Time, and the Cultural Construction of Continuity in Sibog', *Oceania*, 63 (1): 72–86.

Keyes, C. F. (1995), *The Golden Peninsula: Culture and Adaptation in Mainland Southeast Asia*, Honolulu: University of Hawaii Press.

King, V. T. and W. D. Wilder (2003), *The Modern Anthropology of South-east Asia: An Introduction*, London: Routledge.

Kippenberg, H. G. (1998), 'Survivals: Conceiving of Religious History in an Age of Development', in A. L. Molendijk and P. Pels (eds), *Religion in the Making: The Emergence of the Sciences of Religion*, 297–312, Leiden: Brill.

Kirby, D. (2012), 'Occultural *Bricolage* and Popular Culture: Remix and Art in Discordianism, the Church of the SubGenius and the Temple of Psychick Youth', in A. Possamai (ed.), *Handbook of Hyper-real Religions*, 39–57, Leiden: Brill.

Krøijer, S. (2015), 'Figurations of the Future: On the Form and Temporality of Protests among Left Radical Activists in Europe', in L. Meinert and B. Kapferer (eds), *In the Event: Toward an Anthropology of Generic Moments*, 139–52, New York: Berghahn Books.

Kuhn, T. S. (1970), *The Structure of Scientific Revolutions*, 2nd edn, Chicago: University of Chicago Press.

Kuper, A. (1988), *The Invention of Primitive Society: Transformations of an Illusion*, London: Routledge.

Lacan, J. (1977), 'The Signification of the Phallus', in *Ecrits: A Selection*, translated by A. Sheridan, 281–91, London: Routledge.

Laclau, E. (1990), *New Reflections on the Revolution of Our Time*, London: Verso.

Laclau, E. and C. Mouffe (1985), *Hegemony and Socialist Strategy: Towards a Radical Democratic Politics*, London and New York: Verso.

Lahiri, S. (2002), 'Materialising the Spiritual: Christianity, Community, and History in a Philippine Landscape', unpublished PhD diss., Cornell University.

Lahiri, S. (2005), 'The Priestess and the Politician', in A. C. Wilford and K. M. George (eds), *Spirited Politics: Religion and Public Life in Contemporary Southeast Asia*, 23–43, Ithaca, NY: Cornell Southeast Asia Program.

Lakatos, I. (1978), *The Methodology of Scientific Research Programmes*, Cambridge: Cambridge University Press.

Latour, B. (1996), 'On Interobjectivity', *Mind, Culture, and Activity*, 3 (4): 228–45.

Latour, B. (2005), *Reassembling the Social: An Introduction to Actor-Network Theory*, Oxford: Oxford University Press.

Latour, B. (2010), *On the Modern Cult of the Factish Gods*, Durham, NC: Duke University Press.

Lattas, A. (1992a), 'Hysteria, Anthropological Disclosure and the Concept of the Unconscious: Cargo Cults and the Scientisation of Race and Colonial Power', *Oceania*, 63 (1): 1–14.

Lattas, A. (1992b), 'Skin, Personhood and Redemption: The Double Self in West New Britain Cargo Cults', *Oceania*, 63 (1): 27–54.

Lattas, A. (2000), 'Telephones, Cameras and Technology in West New Britain Cargo Cults', *Oceania*, 70 (4): 325–44.

Leach, E. (2004), *Political Systems of Highland Burma: A Study of Kachin Social Structure*, Oxford: Berg.

Leavitt, S. C. (2000), 'The Apotheosis of White Men? A Reexamination of the Beliefs about Europeans as Ancestral Spirits', *Oceania*, 70 (4): 304–23.

Lefebvre, H. (1991), *The Production of Space*, translated by D. Nicholson-Smith, Oxford: Blackwell.

Legge, J. D. (1999), 'The Writing of Southeast Asian History', in N. Tarling (ed.), *The Cambridge History of Southeast Asia Volume I: From Early Times to 1500*, 1–50, Cambridge: Cambridge University Press.

Lévi-Strauss, C. (1955), *Tristes Tropiques*, Paris: Plon.

Lévi-Strauss, C. (1962), *La Pensée Sauvage*, Paris: Plon.

Lévi-Strauss, C. (1966), *The Savage Mind*, London: Weidenfeld and Nicolson.

Lévi-Strauss, C. (1985), 'Race and Culture', in *The View from Afar*, translated by J. Neugroschel and P. Hoss, 3–24, London: Penguin.

Lévi-Strauss, C. (1992), *The Raw and the Cooked: Introduction to a Science of Mythology 1*, translated by J. and D. Weightman, London: Penguin.

Lévi-Strauss, C. (1993a), 'Introduction: History and Anthropology', in *Structural Anthropology Vol. 1*, translated by C. Jacobson and B. G. Schoepf, 1–27, London: Penguin.

Lévi-Strauss, C. (1993b), 'The Structural Study of Myth', in *Structural Anthropology Vol. 1*, translated by C. Jocobson and B. G. Schoepf, 206–31, London: Penguin.

Lévi-Strauss, C. (1994a), 'The Scope of Anthropology', in *Structural Anthropology Vol. 2*, translated by M. Layton, 3–32, London: Penguin.

Lévi-Strauss, C. (1994b), 'Cultural Discontinuity and Economic and Social Development', in *Structural Anthropology Vol. 2*, translated by M. Layton, 312–22, London: Penguin.

Lévi-Strauss, C. (1994c), 'Race and History', in *Structural Anthropology Vol. 2*, translated by M. Layton, 323–62, London: Penguin.

Lévi-Strauss, C. (2001), *Myth and Meaning*, London: Routledge.

Lévi-Strauss, C. (2011), *Tristes Tropiques*, translated by John Weightman and Doreen Weightman. London: Penguin.

Lévi-Strauss, C. and D. Eribon (1991), *Conversations with Claude Lévi-Strauss*, edited by D. Eribon, translated by Paula Wissing, Chicago: University of Chicago Press.

Lindstrom, L. (2004), 'Cargo Cult at the Third Millennium', in H. Jebens (ed.), *Cargo, Cult and Culture Critique*, 15–35, Honolulu: University of Hawaii Press.

Lloyd, G. (1993), *The Man of Reason: 'Male' and 'Female' in Western Philosophy*, 2nd edn, London: Routledge.

Lotringer, S., C. Kraus and H. El Kholti (2007), 'Introduction: Requiem for the Masses', in J. Baudrillard, *In the Shadow of the Silent Majorities*, translated by P. Foss, J. Johnston, P. Patton and A. Berardini, 7–31. Los Angeles: Semiotext(e).

Lubbock, J. (1870), *The Origin of Civilisation and the Primitive Condition of Man: Mental and Social Conditions of Savages*, London: Longmans, Green, and Co.

MacCulloch, D. (2010), *A History of Christianity: The First Three Thousand Years*, London: Penguin.

Malinowski, B. (1922), *Argonauts of the Western Pacific: An Account of Native Enterprise and Adventure in the Archipelagoes of Melanesian New Guinea*, London: Routledge and Kegan Paul.

Malinowski, B. (1984), 'Myth in Primitive Psychology', in idem, *Magic, Science and Religion and Other Essays*, 93–148, Westport, CT: Greenwood Press.

Marasigan, V. (1985), *A Banahaw Guru: Symbolic Deeds of Agapito Illustrisimo*, Manila: Ateneo de Manila University Press.

Marett, R. R. (1912), *Anthropology*, London: Williams and Norgate.

Marett, R. R. (1936), *Tylor*, London: Chapman and Hall.

Marks, J. (1998), *Gilles Deleuze: Vitalism and Multiplicity*, London: Pluto Press.

Marx, K. (1995), 'Preface to *A Critique of Political Economy*', in D. McLellan (ed.), *The Thought of Karl Marx: An Introduction*, 3rd edn, 162–64, London: Macmillan.

McCutcheon, R. T. (1997), *Manufacturing Religion: The Discourse on Sui Generis Religion and the Politics of Nostalgia*, Oxford: Oxford University Press.

McGuire, M. (2008), *Lived Religion: Faith and Practice in Everyday Life*, Oxford: Oxford University Press.

Melitopoulos, A. and M. Lazzarato (2012), 'Machinic Animism', *Deleuze Studies*, 6 (2): 240–49.

Meloni, M. (2014a), 'Biology without Biologism: Social Theory in a Postgenomic Age', *Sociology*, 48 (4): 731–46.

Meloni, M. (2014b), 'How Biology Became Social and What it Means for Social Theory', *The Sociological Review*, 62 (3): 593–614.

Meñez, H. (1999), 'Talismanic Magic and Political Leadership', in H. Meñez, *Explorations in Philippine Folklore*, 95–101, Manila: Ateneo de Manila University Press.

Mertes, T. (2010), 'Anti-Globalization Movements: From Critiques to Alternatives', in B. S. Turner (ed.), *The Routledge International Handbook of Globalization Studies*, 77–95, London: Routledge.

Mesoudi, A., A. Whiten and K. N. Laland (2006), 'Towards a Unified Science of Cultural Evolution', *Behavioural and Brain Sciences*, 29 (4): 329–83.

Mesoudi, A., A. Whiten and K. N. Laland (2007), 'Science, Evolution and Cultural Anthropology', *Anthropology Today*, 23 (2): 18.

Meyer, B. (2010), 'Aesthetics of Persuasion: Global Christianity and Pentecostalism's Sensational Forms', *South Atlantic Quarterly*, 109 (4): 741–63.

Moore, J. D. (2004), *Visions of Culture: An Introduction to Anthropological Theories and Theorists*, 2nd edn, Walnut Creek, CA: Altamira Press.

Morga, A. de. (1970), *History of the Philippine Islands From their Discovery by Magellan in 1521 to the Beginning of the XVII Century. Vols. I–II*, translated by E. H. Blair and J. A. Robertson, New York: Kraus Reprint Co.

Morley, I. (2018), *Cities and Nationhood: American Imperialism and Urban Design in the Philippines, 1898–1916*, Honolulu: University of Hawaii Press.

Mundigo, A. I. and D. P. Crouch (1977), 'The City Planning Ordinances of the Laws of the Indies Revisited', *Town Planning Review*, 48 (3): 247–68.

Nagel, J. (1998), 'Masculinity and Nationalism: Gender and Sexuality in the Making of Nations', *Ethnic and Racial Studies*, 21 (2): 242–69.

Needham, R. (1972), *Belief, Language, and Experience*, Oxford: Basil Blackwell.

Nietzsche, F. (1993), *The Birth of Tragedy out of the Spirit of Music*, translated by S. Whiteside, edited by M. Tanner, London: Penguin.

Nita, M. (2016), *Praying and Campaigning with Environmental Christians: Green Religion and the Climate Movement*, New York: Palgrave Macmillan.

Nongbri, B. (2013), *Before Religion: A History of a Modern Concept*, New Haven, CT: Yale University Press.

Nye, M. (2000), 'Religion, Post-Religionism and Religioning: Religious Studies and Contemporary Cultural Debates', *Method and Theory in the Study of Religion*, 12 (4): 447–76.

Opler, M. E. (1964), 'Cause, Process, and Dynamics in the Evolutionism of E. B. Tylor', *Southwestern Journal of Anthropology*, 20 (2): 123–44.

Orsi, R. A. (2002), *The Madonna of 115th Street: Faith and Community in Italian Harlem, 1880–1950*, 2nd edn, New Haven, CT: Yale University Press.

Ortega, A. A. (2016), *Neoliberalizing Spaces in the Philippines: Suburbanization, Transnational Migration, and Dispossession*, Lanham, MD: Lexington Books.

Otto, T. (2004), 'Work, Wealth and Knowledge: Enigmas of Cargoist Identifications', in H. Jebens (ed.), *Cargo, Cult and Culture Critique*, 209–26, Honolulu: University of Hawaii Press.

Palmer, R. E. (1969), *Hermeneutics: Interpretation Theory in Schleiermacher, Dilthey, Heidegger and Gadamer*, Evanston, IL: Northwestern University Press.

Parsons, T. (1949), *The Structure of Social Action: A Study in Social Theory*, New York: The Free Press.

Partridge, C. (2004), *The Re-Enchantment of the West Vols. I and II*, London: Continuum.

Perraudin, F. (2014), 'Occupy Protestors Forced to Hand Over Pizza Boxes and Tarpaulin', *The Guardian*, 24 October.

Picard, M. (1997), 'Cultural Tourism, Nation-Building, and Regional Culture: The Making of Balinese Identity', in M. Picard and R. E Woods (eds), *Tourism, Ethnicity and the State in Asian and Pacific Societies*, 181–214, Honolulu: University of Hawaii Press.

Primiano, L. N. (1995), 'Vernacular Religion and the Search for Method in Religious Folklife', *Western Folklore*, 54 (1): 37–56.

Putnam, R. D. (2000), *Bowling Alone: The Collapse and Revival of American Community*, New York: Simon and Schuster.

Quibuyen, F. C. (1991), *"And Woman Will Prevail Over Man": Symbolic Sexual Inversion and Counter-Hegemonic Discourse in Mt. Banahaw: The Case of the Ciudad Mistica de Dios*, Manoa: University of Hawaii Centre for Philippine Studies, Occasional Paper No. 10.

Rafael, V. L. (1988), *Contracting Colonialism: Translation and Christian Conversion in Tagalog Society under Early Spanish Rule*, Ithaca, NY: Cornell University Press.

Ram, A. (2014), 'Occupy Protestors to Leave London's Parliament Square', *Financial Times*, 26 October.

Raunig, G. (2010), *A Thousand Machines*, Los Angeles: Semiotext(e).

Reed, R. R. (2002), 'In Quest of a Sustainable Livelihood: Conditions Underlying Ilocano Migrations in the Philippines and Beyond', in H.-H.M. Hsiao, C.-H. Liu and H.-M. Tsai (eds), *Sustainable Development for Island Societies: Taiwan and the World*, 137–78. Taipei: Academia Sinica.

Richman, M. (2003), 'Myth, Power and the Sacred: Anti-Utilitarianism in the Collège de sociologie 1937–9', *Economy and Society*, 32 (1): 29–47.

Rikki (2014), 'Occupy Democracy – The Battle of the Tarpaulin', https://www.indymedia.org.uk/en/2014/10/518468.html.

Robertson, A. (2017), 'Beating the Boundaries: An Exploration of BDSM as Religioning', unpublished PhD diss., Open University.

Rosa, E. A., G. E. Machlis and K. M. Keating (1988), 'Energy and Society', *Annual Review of Sociology*, 14: 149–72.

Rosaldo, R. (1986), 'From the Door of his Tent: The Fieldwork and the Inquisitor', in J. Clifford and G. E. Marcus (eds), *Writing Culture: The Poetics and Politics of Ethnography*, 77–97, Berkeley: University of California Press.

Rovelli, C. (2014), *Seven Brief Lessons on Physics*, translated by S. Carnell and E. Segre, London: Penguin.

Saler, B. (2000), *Conceptualizing Religion: Immanent Anthropologists, Transcendent Natives, and Unbound Categories*, 2nd edn, New York: Berghahn Books.

Sassen, S. (2005), 'The Global City: Introducing a Concept', *Brown Journal of World Affairs*, 11 (2): 27–43.

Schielke, S. and L. Debevec (2012), 'Introduction', in S. Schielke and L. Debevec (eds), *Ordinary Lives and Grand Schemes: An Anthropology of Everyday Religion*, 1–16, New York: Berghahn Books.

Schumacher, J. N. (2009), 'Syncretism in Philippine Catholicism: Its Historical Causes', in J. N. Schumacher, *Growth and Decline: Essays on Philippine Church History*, 107–23, Manila: Ateneo de Manila University Press.

Scott, J. C. (1998), *Seeing Like a State: How Certain Schemes to Improve the Human Condition have Failed*, New Haven, CT: Yale University Press.

Sharpe, E. J. (1986), *Comparative Religion: A History*, 2nd edn, London: Duckworth.

Shatkin, G. (2005), 'Colonial Capital, Modernist Capital, Global Capital: The Changing Political Symbolism of Urban Space in Manila, the Philippines', *Pacific Affairs*, 78 (4): 577–600.

Shukaitis, S., D. Graeber and E. Biddle (2007), *Constituent Imagination: Militant Investigations, Collective Theorisation*, Oakland, CA: AK Press.

Sidel, J. T. (1999), *Capital, Coercion, and Crime: Bossism in the Philippines*, Stanford, CA: Stanford University Press.

Silverman, E. K. (1990), 'Clifford Geertz: Towards a More "Thick" Understanding?', in C. Tilley (ed.), *Reading Material Culture: Structuralism, Hermeneutics and Post-Structuralism*, 121–59, Oxford: Basil Blackwell.

Smith, L. T. (1999), *Decolonising Methodologies: Research and Indigenous Peoples*, London: Zed Books.

Smith, P. and J. C. Alexander (2005), 'Introduction: The New Durkheim', in J. C. Alexander and P. Smith (eds), *The Cambridge Companion to Durkheim*, 1–37, Cambridge: Cambridge University Press.

Soar, K. and P.-F. Tremlett (2017), 'Protest Objects: *Bricolage*, Performance and Counter-Archaeology', *World Archaeology*, 49 (3): 423–34.

Spencer, H. (1890a), 'Transcendental Physiology', in H. Spencer, *Essays: Scientific, Political, and Speculative, Vol. I*, 39–64, London: G. Norman and Son (Reprint: Filiquarian Publishing).

Spencer, H. (1890b), 'The Social Organism', in H. Spencer, *Essays: Scientific, Political, and Speculative, Vol. I*, 157–80, London: G. Norman and Son (Reprint: Filiquarian Publishing).

Spencer, H. (1972), 'Progress: Its Law and Cause', in J. D. Y. Peel (ed.), *Herbert Spencer: On Social Evolution*, 38–52, Chicago: University of Chicago Press.

Sperber, D. (1996), *Explaining Culture: A Naturalistic Approach*, Oxford: Blackwell.

Sperber, D. and L. A. Hirschfeld (2004), 'The Cognitive Foundations of Cultural Stability and Diversity', *Trends in Cognitive Sciences*, 8 (1): 40–46.

Stark, R. and W. S. Bainbridge (1987), *A Theory of Religion*, New York: Peter Lang.

Steenbrink, K. (2003), *Catholics in Indonesia, a Documented History: A Modest Recovery Volume I 1808–1903*, Leiden: KITLV Press.

Steenbrink, K. (2007), *Catholics in Indonesia, a Documented History: The Spectacular Growth of a Self-Confident Minority Volume II 1903–1942*, Leiden: KITLV Press.

Stewart, F. (2017), *Punk Rock is my Religion: Straight Edge Punk and 'Religious' Identity*, London: Routledge.

Steyerl, H. (2017), 'A Sea of Data: Apophenia and Patter (Mis-)Recognition', in H. Steyerl, *Duty Free Art: Art in the Age of Planetary Civil War*, 47–61. London: Verso.

Stiegler, B. (2013), *Uncontrollable Societies of Disaffected Individuals*, translated by D. Ross, Cambridge: Polity.

Stocking, G. W. (1987), *Victorian Anthropology*, New York: The Free Press.

Stocking, G. W. (1995), *After Tylor: British Social Anthropology 1888–1951*, Madison: The University of Wisconsin Press.

Stoddard, B., ed. (2018), *Method Today: Redescribing Approaches to the Study of Religion*, Sheffield: Equinox.

Sturrock, J. (1993), *Structuralism*, London: Fontana Press.

Sturtevant, D. R. (1976), *Popular Uprisings in the Philippines 1840–1940*, Ithaca, NY: Cornell University Press.

Sweet, D. (1970), 'A Proto-Political Peasant Movement in the Spanish Philippines: The *Cofradia de San Jose* and the Tayabas Rebellion of 1841', *Asian Studies*, 8 (1): 94–119.

Tadiar, N. X. M. (1995), 'Manila's New Metropolitan Form', in V. L. Rafael (ed.), *Discrepant Histories: Translocal Essays on Filipino Culture*, 285–313, Manila: Anvil Press.

Tainter, J. A. (1988), *The Collapse of Complex Societies*, Cambridge: Cambridge University Press.

Thomas, A. (2019), 'Auditing in Contemporary Scientologies: The Self, Authenticity, and Material Culture', unpublished PhD diss., Open University.

Thornton, R. J. (1985), '"Imagine Yourself Set Down …": Mach, Frazer, Conrad, Malinowski and the Role of Imagination in Ethnography', *Anthropology Today*, 1 (5): 7–14.

Tilly, C. and S. Tarrow (2015), *Contentious Politics*, 2nd edn, Oxford: Oxford University Press.

Tooby, J. and L. Cosmides (1992), 'The Psychological Foundations of Culture', in J. H. Barkow, L. Cosmides and J. Tooby (eds), *The Adapted Mind: Evolutionary Psychology and the Generation of Culture*, 19–136, Oxford: Oxford University Press.

Tremlett, P.-F. (2008a), *Lévi-Strauss on Religion: The Structuring Mind*, London: Equinox.

Tremlett, P.-F. (2008b), 'False Consciousness and the Jargon of Authenticity: Religion and Nationalism in the Christianized, Lowland Philippines', in R. I. J. Hackett (ed.), *Proselytization Revisited: Rights Talk, Free Markets and Culture Wars*, 83–100, London: Equinox.

Tremlett, P.-F. (2011a), 'Re-cognizing the Mind in the Anthropology of Religion', *NUMEN*, 58 (4): 545–65.

Tremlett, P.-F. (2011b), 'Weber-Foucault-Nietzsche: Uncertain Legacies for the Sociology of Religion', in S. Stern (ed.), *Sects and Sectarianism in Jewish History*, 287–303, Leiden: Brill.

Tremlett, P.-F. (2012), 'Occupied Territory at the Interstices of the Sacred: Between Capital and Community', *Religion and Society: Advances in Research*, 3: 130–41.

Tremlett, P.-F. (2016), 'Affective Dissent in the Heart of the Capitalist Utopia: Occupy Hong Kong and the Sacred', *Sociology*, 50 (6): 1156–69.

Tremlett, P.-F. (2020), 'Effervescence and Implosion in the Sociologies of Emile Durkheim and Jean Baudrillard: Towards a Sociology of Religion at the End of the Social', *International Journal of Baudrillard Studies*, 16 (1), https://baudrillardstudies.ubishops. ca/effervescence-and-implosion-in-the-sociologies-of-emile-durkheim-and-jean-baudrillard-towards-a-sociology-of-religion-at-the-end-of-the-social/.

Tremlett, P.-F., L. T. Sutherland and G. Harvey, eds (2017), *Edward Burnett Tylor, Religion and Culture*, London: Bloomsbury.

Tsing, A. L. (2005), *Friction: An Ethnography of Global Connection*, Princeton, NJ: Princeton University Press.

Tweed, T. (2006), *Crossing and Dwelling: A Theory of Religion*, Cambridge, MA: Harvard University Press.

Tylor, E. B. (1881), *Anthropology: An Introduction to the Study of Man and Civilization*, London: Macmillan and Co.

Tylor, E. B. (1892), 'On the Limits of Savage Religion', *Journal of the Royal Anthropological Institute*, 21: 283–301.

Tylor, E. B. (1903), *Primitive Culture: Researches into the Development of Mythology, Philosophy, Religion, Language, Art and Custom Vols. I and II*, 4th edn, London: John Murray.

Urry, J. (2002), *The Tourist Gaze*, London: Sage.

Walls, A. (2010), 'Christianity', in J. R. Hinnells (ed.), *The Penguin Handbook of the World's Living Religions*, 57–163, London: Penguin.

Walpole, P. (2010), *Learning Sustainable Life: Bukidnon Pulangiyen Community Experience of Integrating Mother Tongue Education for Sustainable Development*, Malaybalay City: Apu Palamguwan Cultural Education Center.

Wanless, C. (2019), 'The Religious and Social Significance of Individualized Religion: Practice Communities and Networks of Transmission in Hebden Bridge', unpublished PhD diss., Open University.

Weber, M. (1978), *Economy and Society: An Outline of Interpretive Sociology Vols. I and II*, edited by G. Roth and C. Wittich. Berkeley: University of California Press.

Weber, M. (1991), 'Science as a Vocation', in H. H. Gerth and C. Wright Mills (eds), *From Max Weber: Essays in Sociology*, 129–56, London: Routledge.

Weber, M. (2002), *The Protestant Ethic and the Spirit of Capitalism*, translated by T. Parsons. London: Routledge.

White, L. A. (1943), 'Energy and the Evolution of Culture', *American Anthropologist*, 45 (3): 335–56.

Whitehouse, H. (2000), *Arguments and Icons: Divergent Modes of Religiosity*, Oxford: Oxford University Press.

Whitehouse, H. (2004), *Modes of Religiosity: A Cognitive Theory of Religious Transmission*, Oxford: Altamira Press.

Wiegele, K. L. (2005), *Investing in Miracles: El Shaddai and the Transformation of Popular Catholicism in the Philippines*, Honolulu: University of Hawaii Press.

Wiegele, K. L. (2006), 'Catholics Rich in Spirit: El Shaddai's Modern Engagements', *Philippine Studies*, 54 (4): 495–520.

Wiegele, K. L. (2011), 'Everyday Catholicism: Expanding the Sacred Sphere in the Philippines', in K. M. Adams and K. A. Gillogly (eds), *Everyday Life in Southeast Asia*, 165–75, Bloomington, IN: Indiana University Press.

Williams, F. E. (1977), 'The Vailala Madness and the Destruction of Native Ceremonies in the Gulf Division', in *'The Vailala Madness' and Other Essays*, edited and with an Introduction by Erik Schwimmer, 331–84, Honolulu: University of Hawaii Press.

Wilson, B. R. (1982), *Religion in Sociological Perspective*, Oxford: Oxford University Press.

Winner, L. (1980), 'Do Artifacts Have Politics?', *Daedalus*, 109 (1): 121–36.

Worsley, P. (1970), *The Trumpet Shall Sound: A Study of Cargo Cults in Melanesia*, 2nd edn, London: Paladin.

Zummer, T. (2012), '… "(medusante)" …', in E. Carels, T. Zummer and K. MacFarlane, *Graphology: Drawing from Automatism and Automation*, 63–83, London: Drawing Room.

INDEX

Lightning Source UK Ltd.
Milton Keynes UK
UKHW051631020920
369185UK00003BA/122